THE INNER DANCE

Other books by Diane Mariechild—

Motherwit: A Guide to Psychic Development.
Crystal Visions: Nine Meditations for Personal and Planetary Peace.

THE INNER DANCE

*A Guide to Spiritual
and Psychological Unfolding*

Diane Mariechild
with Shuli Goodman

The Crossing Press
Freedom, California 95019

Cover design and illustration: Diana Souza
Text art: Susan MacKay, SUMA Designs, Ithaca, N.Y.
Typeset by Bets Ltd., Ithaca N.Y.

Printed in the U.S.A.

Library of Congress Cataloging-in-Publication Data

Mariechild, Diane

   The inner dance: a guide to psychological and spiritual unfolding
/ Diane Mariechild.
      p.   cm.
   Bibliography: p.
   ISBN 0-89594-246-1 : $22.95   ISBN 0-89594-245-3 (pbk.) : $8.95

   1. Spiritual life. 2. Spiritual exercises   I. Title.
BL624.M346 1987
158'. 12--dc19
                                                87-19849
                                                CIP

Acknowledgements

This book is possible through the love and support of many wonderful people, some of whom I wish to honor here. I wish to thank my parents who gave me birth, love and nurturance and who always taught me that "actions speak louder than words." I want to acknowledge my first dancing partners, my brother Robert Sherman and my sisters, Susan Sherman and Barbara Sherman. I am grateful to my sons, Jake and Mike Flaherty, for teaching me love, joy, constancy, caring, and humility. I love you deeply.

The deep clear stream of the Sunray teachings runs through my life and continues to inspire and infuse my work. I am most grateful to Dhyani Ywahoo, my spiritual mother, whose clear, powerful teaching has been a doorway to enter the divine within myself. The lineage that Dhyani carries has provided a wider context for my heart's thoughts and has brought me into deeper relationship with the Earth.

I wish to thank Kate Dunn, my editor at Crossing, who has gone on this journey with me, through all the hills and valleys.

I am most fortunate to have a company of healers, friends who have worked with me to keep me grounded in my body. Thanks and love to my chiropractors, Joan Schneider—for humor, healing hands and a shared love of nature; and Steven Miller, whose gentle, gentle touch brings me greater and greater balance. Thanks for being there and for our loving friendship. I want to acknowledge the wonderful healing hands and heart of a long-time friend and massage therapist, Julie Hobbs. Julie's body work and healing imagery have guided me through several losses. I give my thanks to Patti Stillwater, whose calm, gentle presence is as soothing as her healing touch and whose crystal clear insights provide an integrating force in my life. I am deeply grateful to Bonnie Novakov-Lawlor, who provided massage, wisdom and counsel in a period of spiritual crisis. Bonnie's wonderful movement work,some of which appears herein, has given me greater access to the strength and power of my body.

My love and thanks continue to flow toward "the meditation sisters," my dear friends Linda Hutton and Jean Boughton. For years we have shared heart to heart talks, innumerable travels and stops at many restaurants and other sacred places. Thank you for being my cheerleaders and for loving me. I send sweet love to Nia-Sue Mitchum and Angela Juidici for their vision and insight, for our sleep-overs and long talks about politics, sex, fashion and spirituality. And thanks to Margie Kolchin, sister healer and dharma friend for her love and laughter.

I wish to acknowledge my friends who have shared their writing with me. Thanks to Bronwyn Mills, whose many conversations with me were instrumental in early stages of the manuscript. I want to thank Sejaling, friend of many lifetimes, whose gifts continue over the years, the reading of my manuscript being only one of them. I want to honor Tryna Hope for her delight and exuberance. Her laughter provides a much needed relief and her willingness to read my work and share hers is most appreciated. I want to honor Marcia Black, whose daily phone conversations about writing, philosophy, romance and spirituality have walked me through this book. Marcia's imagery has miraculous healing power, and she introduced me to jazzercise, my favorite mass exercise program.

I wish to extend my love and appreciation to my dear friend Judy Peluso, for years of love and support, for always being ready to "hear my confession." And to Terry Antico—our friendship has endured through so many changes. I am grateful for your reminder, "The Shakti is the teacher."

And I am most grateful for the love and support of my beloved friend and partner, Shuli Goodman, who has provided me with all the above and more, including fashion design. Thanks for your delightful, endearing and humorous companionship, for keeping me in touch with my inner child, for all those wonderful meals, for our deep sharing of ritual and prayer, and for being my colleague on this journey. I am especially grateful for the tremendous amount of work you shared on this manuscript—for the organization, the editing, the many, many hours of discussion and all the emotional support you gave me when I was so exposed, living, as it were, without my skin. I love you. You are the eagle's gift.

Table of Contents

Introduction

To be alive, to know life, is to breathe. To breathe is to move, to move is to change. Movement is fundamental to life. The act of breathing is the automatic act of moving the air, the life force, in and out of the body. The act of breathing is not a separate and isolated act. Every human being breathes. Air infuses this planet and everything upon it. As we breathe in, someone else is breathing out. As we breathe out, someone else is breathing in. We cannot separate the air we breathe from the air someone else breathes. We cannot say, "I will only breathe air that is within three feet of my body." The air is always moving. The air we breathe is shared by millions of beings on this planet. To be alive we are always breathing and this means that we are always changing and that we are always connected.

The principles of change and interconnectedness are the basic premises upon which this book is written. It is my belief that true freedom can be experienced when we acknowledge our connections with all of life and align ourselves with the dynamic movement of the universe. When the connection to all of life is lost or forgotten and/or when people resist or try to force change, many problems arise. Feelings of fear, despair, alienation and loneliness surface when we lose connection with our inner voice. Our lack of connection causes us to disconnect from people and events around us. Seeing others as separate or different, we begin to hold one set of assumptions for ourselves and another for them. In our isolation we begin to distrust other people and out of our distrust come even more limiting patterns of relating — we become fearful and defensive; our bodies tighten and our perception narrows. We fight to maintain our position, protect our property, defend our beliefs. Fearing change, we struggle to create a sense of permanence by looking for the secure job, the best retirement plan, the most compatible partner.

The people I see in my private practice as a therapist and psycho/spiritual counselor and in the workshops I lead throughout the country come to me with common concerns. They feel lonely or afraid, they lack confidence or feel more anger than they can cope with. Some feel out of touch with their feelings or unable to make meaningful connections with others. Some are having problems with their children or partners. Some feel trapped in abusive relationships. Many of them are distraught over the ending of a relationship or the death of someone dear to them. Some people feel their lives or the state of the world are so distressing that they want nothing to do with either.

As I write this the world witnesses the struggle of the Black South Africans to overcome a white fascist regime. The United States government is attempting to force the relocation of Hopi and Navajo people so that multi-national corporations can obtain the coal, oil and uranium discovered under their sacred land. The people of Russia and surrounding countries are struggling to recover from the nuclear power plant disaster at Chernobyl. These particular situations may be new, but the struggles for power, resources and territory are age old problems. We have a highly developed technology and have reached an advanced level of material progress, yet people are still starving. Wars, crime and pollution are universal problems.

We live today with the threat of nuclear destruction. The pace of living has increased so greatly that in one person's lifetime they have seen people travel by horse and buggy and fly on a rocket to the moon. Each one of us, in our own way, is searching for meaning in life. As the winds blow across the earth, carrying from nation to nation the pollution created by the Chernobyl disaster, we may come to realize that Earth has no boundaries. We can place a person here and say this is where one country ends and another begins but, in actuality, we are one people living on one planet. The boundaries we create exist in our minds. We are all people who live on the same planet. We want to be happy, we want to find peace, we want to survive.

Our stories may differ — we each have our own drama that propels us to change. Yet the essence is the same. Sometimes we get caught in the drama of life and, feeling separate, don't see the universality of our challenges. We fail to get to the root of the problems — the feelings of fear and separation that create life's complexities.

We know for certain we are breathing and that life changes. None of us has ever met someone who wasn't born or who won't die. In one moment we can be alive and breathing and in the next moment the breath can cease. Nothing remains the same. It may get "better" or it may get "worse," but it will certainly be different. The big differences we have no trouble noticing — someone close to us dies and we know things are different. Yet the smaller differences whizz past us, unnoticed. It is our tendency to forget the interconnectedness and continual movement of life that makes us shut down in fear, unable to pay attention to our own lives. When we finally allow ourselves to notice, to truly notice, that it could be us who's dead in the very next moment, we become aware of the moment we are in. It suddenly becomes the most precious moment of all, whether it is joyous or painful. We know that it is the only moment we can be sure of.

What will enable us to embrace change? How do we reestablish our connections to the whole circle of life? What can we call upon to transform despair and hardship? How do we find meaning in life? A spiritual practice, a practice of meditation and ritual will enable us to find the inner strength and power to integrate the many life changes. Working with the breath, with movement, with visualization and guided introspection will help us to clear away limitations — the pain, anger and fear that inhibit our self actualization.

The exercises presented in this book are to be worked with again and again. They are designed to take us beyond logical thought into direct experience. Words can never convey the whole meaning; they are the map, not the territory. The truths which have been passed down over many generations through many different spiritual traditions will remain as mere gossip unless they are experienced in the heart, on a very deep level — beyond words, beyond analysis.

You may think of this book as a workbook, a manual, a guide to life. Some of the exercises speak to specific issues while others are designed to develop awareness of the energy of the present moment. All of them will be useful in understanding a basic truth of life — everything in this universe exists within a relationship that is continually moving and changing. "The universe is a dance of energy, a universe, a single song of everchanging rhythms and harmonies."[1] When you open to the inner dance it will transform your life. Practicing the exercises in this book will encourage that opening. You will learn to strengthen and trust the intuition as you still the mind and listen to the inner voice. You will discover ways of releasing or transforming negative beliefs. You will bring the female, male and child energy within you into balance. Your communication with others will become clearer and stronger. When you are freed of inner conflicts, you are able to fully express all that you are and this brings a great sense of joy and peace.

We learn through direct experience that a global concern is a personal concern and personal concerns are also global concerns. Everyone we meet will at some time suffer grief or loss and everyone we meet wants to live in peace. No one wants a nuclear war. No one wants to see their children go hungry. No matter how different we appear on the outside, inside we have similar feelings, fears, hopes and dreams. As you work with these exercises you will discover your true self, your true nature. And when you uncover this true self, you will find that it exists in everyone. When we really let ourselves "see" ourselves, we find that we can "see" the self in everyone we meet. The inner dance is the pulse of the universe that exists within our hearts. The awakened dancer moves to that pulse. This book is an invitation for you to discover the inner dance.

I
How to Use This Book

Everything within the universe is connected and in a continual process of change. Our understanding of the principles of interrelatedness and change have an enormous impact on the way in which we view ourselves and the world. When we are able to truly perceive that we are dancers in a universe of dancing light, then we will experience peace and freedom. The succeeding chapters offer a variety of visualization exercises, physical exercises and rituals designed to uncover our own innate wisdom through opening us to a sense of an integral connection with all of life.

Play with the exercises. Be gentle and kind to yourself as you begin to explore who you are. Work slowly and patiently so that you can find the gift in every situation you encounter. You will discover that life can be transformed from a series of seemingly unrelated and painful events to a kaleidoscope of challenges, colorfully designed to show the power of love.

The exercises are simple, yet powerful, so you may find that strong emotions or memories surface during an exercise, immediately after or, sometimes, several hours or days later. A natural grieving process may also take place as painful memories and feelings of loss and scarcity are released. These experiences are all a part of the process so give yourself some space for these exercises. This may mean not planning to work with an exercise immediately prior to being active in the world. It definitely means being patient and loving towards yourself, knowing that you have all the time you need to make the changes you need to make. You have the right to experience whatever emotions you experience without shame or guilt. You are fine just the way you are, and it is also fine to make changes. If you feel the need for grounding after an exercise, some of these things may help: breathing deeply and exhaling through your mouth, washing your hands, shaking the excess energy from your hands and placing them palms down on the floor, massaging your feet, splashing your face and neck with cool water, doing some physical exercise, drinking a glass of water or juice or having a cup of tea, having something light to eat, writing in your journal, or talking with a friend.

Make the time in which you explore special by creating a calm, peaceful environment. You may want to make an altar as a place of focus. The altar can be as simple or as ornate as you wish. Be mindful of the objects you select to be part of your altar. As you tenderly care for each sacred object, you are caring for life, itself. Have each of the elements represented on the altar: a candle for fire, incense for air, some salt for the Earth, a small bowl of water. Crystals, stones or other special objects are appropriate for an altar. If there is a particular understanding you are seeking or a particular situation or feeling you want to transform, you may include on the altar an object to represent it. You might, for example, want to place on your altar a picture of a loved one for whom you are grieving, or perhaps a special pen to symbolize the writer within you, or maybe a feather to represent your power to soar.

Many people in this modern day and age feel that taking time to refresh oneself is selfish, or that exercises, meditations and rituals won't work or are simply a waste of time. These ideas, even when not consciously believed, can create some underlying doubt or guilt. Initially, making the time to do the exercises may be more challenging than the actual work itself. Affirmations can help in this instance. You may want to say to yourself several times during the day, "I have the time and the energy to do visualizations every day," or something similar that you make up yourself. It is important to remember the full circle of life. As we feed and nourish ourselves we are also feeding our friends and families. Each time we find peace and clarity within ourselves, that peace and clarity can be felt by and shared with everyone we meet. A wonderful way to begin these exercises is to dedicate your unfolding clarity to the good of all life. This is a Buddhist practice called dedicating the merit. Whatever good is gained for the individual is dedicated for the benefit of all life.

The visualization exercises in this book can be placed in two categories. The first category I would call awareness exercises. They are found primarily in Chapters Three and Four. They explore the breath, sensations and feelings in the body, and thoughts and images in the mind. Their purpose is to bring our focus into the present moment, whether that moment is joyful or painful. In bringing our awareness into the present we see how quickly the moment changes. Our work is to be with that moment, that image, that thought or sensation, without trying to change it, judge it, or hang onto it.

The second category of visualizations are those that work with the specific content of our lives. Here we take a still photograph, so to speak, of one of the many incidents in our lives. It may be the death of a parent, a conflict with a friend, or our fear of changing occupations. We know that everything is moving and changing, yet we decide to stop the motion picture and investigate a chosen situation or belief.

Both of these ways of working are important in awakening the dancer, in encouraging ourselves to join the dance. We need to learn patience, to open ourselves to the moment without critical judgement. We need to trust and to let go of whatever it is that we cling to. We can learn to do this using both methods: we can release fear without trying to determine *what* it is that we are afraid of, *why* we are afraid or *when* our fear first began. We can also work with fear through specific issues, releasing or transforming our pain, affirming the harmony, strength and love we all long for.

We can work with visualizations to create the kind of life we want. We can set clear intentions and plan what we want to actualize today, next month or next year.

The exercises in this book are written so that they can be worked with individually, with a partner, or in a group. When you are working alone be sure to read the explanation and the exercise through several times so that you have an understanding of what you are going to do before you begin. You may want to record some of the exercises on a cassette tape and play them back to guide yourself.

When you work with a friend you can take turns guiding each other. This is especially important in doing the work which involves transformation of painful experiences. Be sure to choose someone with whom you feel comfortable, who is able to be present, yet maintain a sense of detachment so that she will not interfere in your healing process. This detachment can be maintained through meditative attention on the part of the guide. It would be wise for the one guiding to start out with the "Earth and Sky" meditation as a grounding. Dedicating the work also affirms our connection with the full circle of life and is a good way of grounding and centering.

The guide should read the words slowly so that there is time for them to be deeply experienced. A calm, gentle voice is an aid to meditative attention. While guiding, be sensitive to your own inner responses as well as to those of your friend. If you begin to feel overwhelmed, it may be that your friend is also feeling overwhelmed. You can help her move through her feelings by breathing deeply and staying clear. Silently affirm her wholeness, her ability to transform, to heal, to be one with all life. Remember to maintain receptivity without judging experiences as "good" or "bad." If your friend wishes to stop the exercise before it is complete, or if she is experiencing painful feelings, it may be helpful to suggest an affirmation of her wholeness, to affirm that what she is experiencing is a state of mind that will always change. When she is ready to stop, suggest that the images and feelings she is experiencing dissolve. Then guide her back to her usual awareness with the affirmation: "You are wide awake and filled with peaceful and loving energy." If further grounding is necessary, suggest she use one or more of the grounding techniques suggested earlier, such as shaking excess energy from her hands or massaging her feet.

When using the visualizations with a group you may want to choose two people to act as guides. One guide can read the exercises to the group and the other can help to keep the energy clear by sitting in meditation. The "Earth and Sky" meditation is very appropriate for this purpose. Both guides can do the "Earth and Sky" meditation together before beginning the group; then one guide can continue with it throughout the exercises. Working with a group is an excellent opportunity to affirm all the voices in the circle. Each person has something to share with the group and something to learn from the group. We become like mirrors for each other, reflecting the wisdom that is within us. Working together we have more energy and resources to amplify the patterns that are harmonious and to release or transform the patterns that are limiting. In a group we have the love and support we need to work through our fears and pains. The group can remind us to be patient, to have a sense of humor, and to remember that everything is within us. The circle is affirmed when we begin and end group work by joining hands and sitting in silence, or chanting together, or by doing both — first chanting, then sitting in silence.

Physical exercises are most challenging to write about. They are more easily understood when demonstrated. Nonetheless, I have included physical exercises in this book because I believe awakening is, to a large extent, an "in the body" experience.

I have also included a number of rituals. I offer them as suggestions and as examples of how rituals can be structured. Read through them, try the ones that appeal to you and remember that you can adapt them to fit your needs or you can create entirely new ones. The grounding suggestions given previously are important here also. And I'd like to add one reminder about attitude: we need to maintain a sense of awe, of wonder and mystery about the universe. As human beings we cannot be fully aware of all the consequences of our acts. We are connected in marvelous ways that are not perceptible to us in the present. The energy we send out goes on and on and on. We need to take time to think what we are doing and why we are doing it. It is our choice whether our thoughts and actions are those which affirm the connection to all life or those that negate it. Think of rituals as honoring the life connections and perform the rituals in a way that will do good for all of life.

II
Awakening the Dancer

Images serve as windows within the psyche, they resonate with a
multiplicity of meanings. When these images are glistening stones in the
river of eros, their power to heal and transform is miraculous, for this river
of eros comes from the heart and returns, once again, to the heart.
So beauty can absorb and transform sorrow and pain,
for beauty is the heart's language.

—Marcia Black

The image of the awakened dancer holds enormous power for me. It is my way of both describing and accessing the universal knowledge of the heart. The dancer is the wisdom self whose love, power and grace infuse our life and the lives of all those we touch. The dancer moves; she changes. Aware of her relationship to time and space, she moves through all dimensions, giving context and meaning to life. The dancer is the personification of our natural rhythm and creativity; she is the spark of creation itself. When the dancer awakens, we are open to seeing, beyond the physical form, the greater being that we are.

When we awaken we experience a heightened awareness of the interconnectedness of all of life. The rigid separations and definitions that have kept us isolated and afraid fall away; the artificial boundaries dissolve and the authentic self emerges. The awakened heart is without fear. We are able to see a part of ourselves in everyone and everyone as a part of ourselves. All phenomena are recognized as manifestations of a basic oneness. The knowledge of the underlying unity or connection of all life is expressed in modern physics which sees the universe as a dance of subatomic particles. Nothing in the universe is solid, separate or static. The essence of matter is energy, tiny dancing particles in constant, fluid motion. This dance of energy, this dance of light that physicists describe as the phenomena of particles and waves can be understood metaphorically as our individuality (the particles) and our relationship, our unity (the waves). This perpetual motion creates webs of light that continually interpenetrate and interrelate. This dance of light is the universe making love to itself.

The acknowledgement of the inherent unity and connectedness of life is also expressed in the world view of many mystical and spiritual traditions. It is seen in the sacred art of these traditions from the mandala of Eastern religions to the medicine wheel of the Native Americans. We live in a universe of reciprocal relationships, where we all are part of the amazing dance of light. Sub-atomic physics tells us that this energy cannot be created or destroyed. It simply changes form. We are connected individuals and we can trace our connection back to the dawn of the universe. From fertile darkness, the primal womb, came a burst of starlight. Everything in the universe shared that beginning. The hydrogen atoms that were formed in that starlight have been transformed throughout the millenia. We are from the stars, the ancient materials that were a part of that primeval fireball have been recycled to form our bodies.

Our survival as a species depends on the understanding of relationship. We are born with an original creative spark that connects us to the whole circle of life just as the genes we carry connect us to a particular family. This spark is the divine within us, the original and recycled hydrogen atom. To awaken we must rekindle this spark. We must nurture it until it becomes a glowing light that guides all of our actions. In a universe of reciprocal relationship, we each have a part in creation. Every action affects, and is affected by, every other action. This knowledge calls forth our personal responsibility — we each must take part in creating a life that is good for all the Earth.

The inability to sense connection, the refusal to take responsibility that dominates personal life as well as national policy comes from the notion of separation. The concept of separation breeds fear and fear is presently so widespread and deeply ingrained in us that we have all collaborated in the creation of weapons that can kill each person twenty times over. If we are to survive as a species we must transform the concept of separation and the fear that springs from it. It is fear that prevents us from seeing the totality of every moment. It limits our perceptions, creates judgements and causes further separation.

Where does fear originate? Buddhist philosophy traces fear back to the original split between "I" and "others." When we believe in the existence of "me" and "my space" and "you" and "your space," we have created a separation. There is a constant struggle between "my space" and "your space." We try to resolve this by making "my space" larger. But the more we attempt to make "my space" bigger, the wider becomes the gap between the "me" and the "you."

The struggle becomes more and more involved and is acted out in many of life's dramas. Eventually we forget the original split. We simply see everything in life as good or bad, safe or unsafe. We spend enormous amounts of time and energy trying to pull the good and safe toward us and trying to push away the bad and unsafe. If something is seen as neither good nor bad, we act indifferently toward it. Our lives revolve around complex variations on these three themes. Each variation is an attempt to protect ourselves, to control our environment, to eliminate pain. Yet all the pain we experience, in whatever form it takes, originates from these three themes which are responses to the original idea of separation, the idea of "us" and "them."[1]

What will free us from pain? The realization that everything in life is impermanent, changing, unstable is the only thing that can eventually free us from pain. If we are attached to something staying the same, we experience pain when it changes. If we are too attached to people, we act possessively and attempt to run their lives even though we know this does not work and only creates more conflict. Sometimes we become attached to material objects in the mistaken belief that by acquiring more we will find happiness. What can happen is that we spend years in unsatisfying jobs to pay for all the things that are supposed to keep us comfortable. Sometimes we feel certain places or situations will bring us freedom. But even those places of seeming safety can eventually become traps. Many people become attached to particular ideas, thoughts or perceptions of themselves or other people. Although identifying labels and concepts can be valuable, sometimes giving us more freedom, we must take care not to become attached to a particular perception, for when our perceptions become fixed and rigid they begin to cause pain. Attachment, whether it is to people, things, places or ideas, simply doesn't bring happiness. Freedom comes when we learn to live in loving association with people and are able to let go of things when they outgrow their usefulness. We experience freedom when we are able to share our love, ideas and material resources and when we appreciate the places we visit and the ideas we hold and, yet, can leave them without regret. In essence, freedom comes from letting go. "Freedom," as Janis Joplin sang some years ago, "is just another word for nothing left to lose."

When we are attached to something, we are unable to connect to the world. Without the connection there is separation and fear, and therefore, the experience of pain. When we let go of the attachment just a little, we have a little freedom and when we let go a lot we have a lot of freedom. When we let go completely, then there is complete freedom. Most people want freedom, yet most people have a difficult time letting go. We want to be happy. We don't want to suffer, so why can't we let go? Why can't we be like the tree who loses her leaves each autumn and has new growth each spring?

We are afraid. What are we afraid of? Most people fear letting go and this letting go or change is the fear of death. Many people view death as the final annihilation and each letting go as a death of sorts. Every loss takes a part of us and we feel more empty and alienated. We may try to fill this emptiness by holding on to whatever we think will fill that emptiness. In trying to protect ourselves from more loss we create more attachments and the feeling of separation becomes stronger. The pain of this separation is exacerbated by our concept of linear reality. We see experiences as occurring one after the other in a random way; we miss the subtle connections that underlie all of life's events. While linear thought is necessary for us to communicate it is not a criterion for reality.

We are separated from the wisdom of our true nature, and often fail to sense and honor our connectedness. We long to connect but we do not acknowledge the longing. Or, if we do, we don't know what we long for so that our longing becomes twisted. We are caught in the bind of either dependence or independence. The union we seek is the union of the divine/creative nature within ourselves. The death that we grieve is the loss of the memory of this divine/creative connection. Our journey through life is the journey to remember, to reconnect.

Women hold the key to remembering. Women generally experience a greater awareness of interconnectedness than do men. However, because we are all born of women, both women and men carry the knowledge of interconnectedness. This primal wisdom remains buried within, lost to our conscious awareness. Separated from the knowledge of our collective origin, fear arises. If this fear is not recognized and transformed it is projected outward where it turns to greed, hatred, grief or rage. This fear can become institutionalized as a system of thought and thus the "isms" are born. The root of all "isms," whether racism, sexism, classism or anti-Semitism, is fear. This fear allows us to treat the "other" with a different set of standards. The other is not treated with the same respect, sensitivity and caring as those who are perceived to be the same. The other is not given access to equal opportunities and resources.

We are the particle and we are the wave. This is a time of integration, of building bridges, of recognizing that we are connected individuals. We can no longer translate our unity into uniformity nor can we use our differences as weapons to destroy each other. Eastern culture, Western culture, political activists, meditators, women, men, gays, lesbians and heterosexuals, people of every race: we all have something to share, something to learn from one another.

We are living in a time of great upheaval and change. "According to the Tsalagi (Cherokee) calendar, we are in the ninth stage of purification, a time to transform attitudes of aggression and scarcity to right relationship and balance. The people and the land are one, in a bioresonant relationship. For the people and the planet to survive, a change in thought is called for."[2]

The thought of separation is an illusion. The reality is a universe of changing, reciprocal relationships. We find this truth whether we study quantum physics or practice Buddhist meditation. We live in a universe of dancing light with all living things shining like stars in a vast sky, connected by wondrous and unseen forces. We have the choice to awaken, to respond to the inner dance, the energy of the universe flowing through us.

This time of great change offers us many opportunities. Change involves some degree of discomfort. Yet, when we look back, we can see that we have done most of our growing during times of upheaval and change. It is these periods of change, in fact, that often precede an awakening. It is as though on some deep level the psyche knows there must be an upheaval to shake loose the habitual patterns. In times of unbearable pain or during the suffering that accompanies death, the heart is torn open so we can no longer cling to the familiar. In that open space we seek new meaning. Sometimes the awakening causes a complete transformation. Other times, change is more subtle. Yet, the experience is profound — it alters our perceptions of the world.

Awakening does not have to be preceded by a trauma, whether sudden or gradual. We can awaken when we are touched by the magnificence of nature, as in the viewing of a brilliant red/orange sunset. We may feel a particular piece of music deep within our bones or we may feel our hearts open in loving. We may find that awakening occurs gradually as we care for an animal or a plant. Awakening can come through any experience that allows us to move beyond our limited perceptions.

Some dear friends decided last year to set aside ten months in their lives to walk across the country for peace. In the long months of walking, through all kinds of weather, meeting all kinds of people, they discovered love. Every person they met, in spite of the many different stories they shared, wanted peace and love. The peacewalkers found their stereotypes shattered, one by one, as they walked. They left behind negative feelings, expectations of how things "should" be, and their ideas of separateness. It is a joy to be around Patty and Mary. They have learned how to access their own strength and resources. They are peace. It comes from making that choice every day, in everything they do.

Awakening is the harmony that comes when we realize oneness and are motivated to work for the good of all. Stephen Levine[3] likens the process of awakening to that of fruit ripening on a tree. It ripens slowly, day by day, until it is fully ripe and falls from the tree. Even that awakening, which seems sudden, needed all those instances that preceded it to makes it ripe. "Any moment could enlighten us if we would see its totality, its complexities, its simpleness. It seems to take awhile before we clear the senses enough, clear our conditioning enough to let go of models and perceptions so that we can simply hear, simply see, perceive deeply enough to understand the way things are."[4] As the dancer awakens within each being, we will together create a world of peace.

III
Foundations

By opening ourselves, surrendering ourselves, we may know the reality, or spirits, of many things.... As we bring ourselves in resonance with these spirits, align our own centers with them; they may talk to us, teach us, guide us, protect us, help us, and endow us with The Power that is manifest in them.

A thing of power is given its power through our recognition in it of the Power that flows through everything — it is given its holy power through the power of our consciousness, which is not ours, but of the Great Spirit.

—Gayle High Pine

Human life begins with our first breath and ends with our last. What exists in the passage between these breaths is the opportunity to explore, to learn and to experience what life is all about. One of life's certainties is change. It is easy enough to see that life is change. We can observe a tree as it goes through the seasons, watch the moon as it waxes and wanes, or follow the ebb and flow of the tides. We find it more challenging, however, to accept ourselves as part of changing nature.

We are a part of nature, yet, by our ruthless destruction of nature we have severed ourselves from our own inner selves. In our rush for material and technological advancements, we have created an ever-widening split between body and mind. In subduing nature we have subdued a part of ourselves. We have set ourselves apart from the Earth and apart from the dark, maternal consciousness. Our bodies have become a battleground of reason *versus* instinct and emotion. We can return to our essential nature and heal the split between body and mind by observing the movement of our breath and listening to the invisible breath, the spirit of the Earth.

Focusing on the breath, learning to sense our connection with Earth and sky, and strengthening our physical body as a temple in which the spirit can manifest gives us the foundation for a spiritual practice. These three disciplines can comprise a complete daily meditation practice. A spiritual practice is a way of accessing the divine creativity that exists inside each of us. It is a process of finding our own strength and balance, of celebrating, with sound and silence, the essence of who we are. To realize ourselves as authentic spiritual beings takes a lot of physical and emotional stamina. We must be willing to face our fears and doubts.We must work to transform any feelings of separation we may hold. We must overcome any laziness or irresponsibility that is still with us. Beneath each of these states lies enormous reservoirs of love, power and authenticity, and the ability to deeply and honestly respond to life.

As human life begins with the breath, we begin our practice with the breath. The word "inspire" means to breathe. To breathe in, inspiration — to fill with spirit. Most of us do not breathe fully. We do not bring the breath fully into the body and this means we do not bring the spirit fully into the body. Unless we begin to breathe deeply we will be unable to actualize our full human potential on a physical level, complete breathing enables us to fully oxygenize the blood, which, in turn, feeds all the organ systems in the body. On a spiritual level, breath is the life force energy that flows through us.[1]

The sharing of breath is the sharing of life. The air that you exhale, I inhale.[2] Breathing is one of our connections with all human beings. We live on the same planet; we breathe the same air; the same sun shines upon us. Recognizing our deep interconnections with all life is an integral part of our spiritual practice. It is a spiritual practice in itself. The universal connection, the balance of life, depends on a natural give and take. Each individual must recognize her relationship to the whole, what she is giving and what she is receiving. The cycle of respiration (breathing in and breathing out) is both the most basic act of reciprocity performed by humans and a metaphor for all the patterns of reciprocity we experience. Trees and other growing plants take in carbon dioxide and give off oxygen; humans (as well as other animals) breathe in oxygen and give off carbon dioxide. Without this cycle, neither we nor the plants could live.

"To walk in balance" is an expression Native Americans use to acknowledge our connection with and responsibility for the Earth. The "Earth and Sky" meditations in this book build a foundation for understanding this concept. To walk in balance we must have our feet planted firmly on the ground and we must bring our consciousness fully into our bodies. To do this it is necessary to strengthen the physical body. Many people who are drawn to psychic, psychological or spiritual work tend to forget the need for physical strength and grounding, their lack of familiarity with their bodies amplifying the body/mind split.

The physical exercises in this chapter help us to develop a strong and stable base, so that we have more movement and flexibility. We need strong feet and legs to carry the weight of our bodies. Our bodies compensate for a lack of support from our feet and legs, or from our spines, in ways that may create misalignments. When the chest is not supported by the base of the body, it closes in an attempt to stabilize and protect itself. A closed chest and hunched shoulders make a closed heart. To open the heart, to experience the actuality of love, we need to feel safe and supported. This safety comes through the movement of the breath, and the building of a strong base of support in the physical body.

Breathe Free

Breathing is basic to life. We can live for weeks without food, for days without water, but only a few minutes without breathing. Breathing, unlike walking, talking or eating, does not need our conscious awareness. Breathing occurs even while we are sleeping. When we learn to become conscious of our process of breathing we are uniting the conscious and the unconscious. If we really understand and experience the profound significance of the breath, it will teach us more than all the philosophies in the world.

The movement of the breath can be seen as a metaphor for life. Breath, like life, is always moving, going in and out, constantly changing. If we can become comfortable with the constant change that is happening every moment within our bodies, then perhaps we can learn something that will enable us to find security and comfort through all of life's changes. The enormous fear that we are experiencing at this time on the planet, fear for our very survival, has affected this most basic function — breathing. We have come to accept chest breathing as normal when, in actuality, it is a survival mechanism expressing the "fight or flight" syndrome. The natural breathing pattern is a full breath, deep in the belly. This is the way a baby breathes.

Breath is spirit. To inspire is to be filled with breath, to be filled with spirit. When we breathe deeply we are inspired, filled with the creative energy of life. In this exercise we become witness to the act of breathing. The secret of meditation is that we become what we meditate upon. We meditate on the breath and we become the breath, one with the spirit, the movement of life.

This exercise can be practiced from fifteen minutes to an hour or more. Your spiritual practice could be based on this exercise done daily throughout your whole life.

Sit comfortably with your spine erect. In a relaxed way, bring your attention to your breath. Watch the breathing. Are you aware of the breath entering your nostrils? Where does this awareness begin? How deep is your breath? Watch it travel through your body. Is it shallow and quick? Is it slow and deep? Just watch your breath as though you never realized that you were breathing. This is new. Breathing is happening and you are watching it.

Breathing in and breathing out. Breathing in and breathing out.

Now begin to play with your breath. Make it rapid and shallow. After breathing this way for a minute or two, try slowing the breath. Inhale, pause, and then exhale. Inhale, pause, and then exhale. See how the breath changes. See if you feel anything different in any part of your body. Now let your breath move in and out slowly, without pausing. Inhale and exhale. Inhale and exhale. Inhale and exhale.

Playing with the breath. Experimenting, observing, playing with the breath. Now, imagine that you are inhaling light and that, as you exhale, your breath, in the form of light, moves out through the palms of your hands. Inhale light and exhale light through your palms.

Inhaling and exhaling, gently playing with the breath. Continue to imagine your breath as light moving through you and, as you exhale, imagine that you are exhaling through the space between your shoulder blades. Now, continuing to breathe deeply, imagine that, as you exhale, the breath is leaving through the soles of your feet. Pay close attention to your body. Does it feel the same? Does it feel different?

Breathe in and breathe out. Breathe in and breathe out. Now let the breath flow freely, without attempting to hasten or slow it. Watch the breath. Inhale and exhale. Inhale and exhale. Notice how you feel. Is it different or is it the same as when you began this exercise?

When you are ready open your eyes.

Earth and Sky I

The exercise "Earth and Sky" is inspired by my practice of the Sunray Meditation.[3] Native Americans have much to teach us about our connection with the Earth.To Native Americans, the Earth is a living entity, the mother of all life. All her children, all the things in nature are alive — the rocks, the trees, the animals, the people. Everything is united in one harmonious whole. My teacher, Dhyani Ywahoo, says, "The Earth is alive and She sings and She calls us to recall again our sacred place and our dance in this life. She calls us to recognize that all of us walk around the sacred wheel."

The experience of the Earth energy as a tangible feeling may be a new awareness for people. To help in this understanding, think of a time in your life when you were particularly touched by the beauty of the Earth. It may have been the power of the ocean's waves crashing against the rocks, the stillness of a clear lake, the sweet breath of a forest, or the pulsing heat and color of the desert sand that moved you. Even life-long city dwellers can recall being moved by the shade of a tree in a park, a tiny patch of grass, or a spring flower in a window box. The vibrations of Earth, of nature, are real and we are receiving them in the form of energy all the time, even through concrete sidewalks. In the beginning we may have to imagine this energy but, through continued practice, we will become sensitive to its constant pulse.

To help us in visualizing the energy of the Earth, it is a good idea to gather some rocks and spend a little time looking at their varied textures and colors. When we hold these colors clearly in our mind, it will be easy to visualize the hot, molten rock in the center of the Earth. This rock is pulsing and sending forth waves of energy which we are always receiving.

We are receiving energy from the sky at the same time that the energy from the Earth is vibrating through us. When we really ground ourselves and feel our connection to Earth, the stable base we have created in our bodies opens us to receiving the energy of the sky. Like the rays of the sun, it is ever streaming down upon us.

We can imagine the energy of the sky as a blessing pouring down from above, touching us gently. Some people visualize it as a golden light, others as a soft violet, others as a white light. It is important to ground the mind energy, to cool it down in order to lessen the "burn-out" that so many people experience these days. Draw the sky energy into your body only to the degree that it is comfortable for you. As we strengthen we are able to channel stronger and stronger vibrations. Sensing these cooler colors, like violets and blues, in the upper body helps bring us into balance. The "Earth and Sky" meditation affirms our connection with the universe. It is a meditation that can be done again and again. Along with the "Breathe Free" meditation, it can become a lifelong spiritual practice. You may get a sense of the energy flowing through you in a few minutes or you may want to work slowly, making this a meditation that lasts from twenty minutes to an hour. You may want to stand to do this meditation so that you really get a sense of the Earth beneath your feet.

> Imagine yourself standing on a beautiful spot somewhere upon the Earth. Feel your feet firmly on the ground. Let the weight of your body be balanced equally on both feet. Feel the strength in your abdomen as you pull it slightly in and up. Let your shoulders move down and back so there is no feeling of tension in them. Feel the weight of your arms and hands hanging comfortably at your sides. Let your head rest easily on your neck. Your eyes are clear and bright as you look out across the beautiful land.
>
> Imagine a huge rock deep in the center of the Earth. Visualize the texture and color of this rock. See the deep, rich earthen colors. Know that the rock is alive, the Earth

is alive, you are alive. Imagine the life force energy vibrating from that rock and spiraling upward from the center of the Earth. Feel this energy as a gentle pulse. See it as waves of light. Hear it as a steady beat.

Now focus on your breathing and, as you inhale, imagine that you are inhaling the waves of light that are spiraling upward from the heart of the Earth. Feel the pulse of the Earth. This pulse is very subtle, yet very powerful. Feel a warmth or tingling sensation as the energy of the Earth travels up through the soles of your feet. As you inhale imagine the life force energy of the Earth moving up through your feet and traveling up through your ankles, calves, knees and thighs. Breathe slowly and deeply and, with each inhalation, draw the Earth energy up through your feet and legs into your pelvis. Feel the warmth and tingling as the Earth energy fills your pelvis. Imagine, sense, or feel this energy moving deeply within your body.

And, now, imagine it traveling up your spine. You may want to imagine your spine extending down into the Earth, like a root or a tail to receive the Earth energy. Feel, sense, imagine the deep connection with the Earth. You are being fed and nourished by the energy of the Earth. Inhale the Earth energy and, as you exhale, imagine it flowing out the top of your head and washing over you as it returns to the Earth.

Sense the full circle of energy as you are fed by the Earth and the energy returns to the Earth. Receiving and giving, giving and receiving — the full circle of energy. Continue to inhale and exhale, to be fed by the energy of the Earth. Sense, know, and feel yourself as a part of the Earth as the Earth energy flows to you and through you. Feel your feet firmly grounded upon the Earth. You are alive. You are in your body. You are breathing.

Standing upon the Earth, breathing the Earth. As you are breathing in the Earth, the sky is above your head. High up in the vast sky is the sun shining its warm, golden light down upon you. As you breathe in, feel the golden sunlight washing down upon you. Feel the energy of the sky vibrating around you. Waves of light flowing down, filling your head and traveling down through your body. As you breathe in, the life force energy of the sky is being drawn into your body. Inhale, breathing in the energy of the sky. Feel it flowing through you, out through the soles of your feet and back up into the sky. The energy is coming from and returning to the sky. You are receiving energy from the sky.

As you continue to breathe in and out, in and out, energy from the Earth and energy from the sky is flowing to you and through you. Earth and sky, Earth and sky. You are one with the Earth and sky.

Earth and Sky II

"Earth and Sky II" is a deepening of the Earth and Sky" meditation. It includes specific focus on the chakras[4] — the energy
centers in the body. This exercise works with the alignment and
integration of these centers. Chakra is the Sanskrit word for the
wheel-like vortices of energy that exist along the surface of the
etheric body. The etheric body is the invisible double of the physical body. It interpenetrates the physical body and extends slightly
beyond it. It functions to keep the physical body alive through
the absorption and distribution of the streams of universal
light/energy. The energy centers are in perpetual motion, drawing
in the life force from the universal field of energy. As the individual's development unfolds, the chakras spin more rapidly,
pulsing with light, so that greater and greater amounts of energy can pass through them.

The number and location of the chakras differ slightly according to the system or culture one is working within. Some cultures describe only two and others between six and twenty. Seven
seems to be an average number. In location they correspond to
the endocrine glands in the physical body. Many systems recognize centers in the hands and feet and some say there are centers
several feet below and above the physical body. In the "Earth
and Sky" meditation, I am working with seven chakras. As you
begin to work both with this meditation and with the physical
exercises that follow it, trust your own experience regarding the
location of the chakras. Each system may be thought of as a
metaphor, so allow your experience to find the metaphor that
works for you.

Each chakra relates to a different aspect of life. As we release
fear and limitation, the chakras open and we have more access
to universal energy. The root chakra, located at the base of the
spine, is the chakra connected with the basic grounding of the

body. It is in this area that we acknowledge the body as our own body. The root chakra has to do with who we are as a physical entity. This includes our racial identity as well as the physicality of sex. All issues that have to do with physical survival and security such as housing, money and physical prosperity are related to the root chakra. It is in this chakra that we claim our right to exist, to allow the self to have a home. People who have suffered physical and sexual abuse will need to strengthen this center because the emotional impact of the abuse gives the message, "You don't have the right to exist. You don't have the right to control your own body. Your body is not safe."

The navel chakra, which is located slightly below the umbilicus, is related to the emotional and merging aspect of sexuality. It is from this center that we can feel another person's pain or joy. If we absorb too much energy from others without releasing it, we will compulsively try to solve their problems. This never works because a person's problems can be solved only by that person. Connecting with others in this compulsive manner keeps us attached in a limiting way and leads to the creation of addictive patterns of relating. The only solution for this is to discharge the other person's energy from our bodies. One of the ways to gain choice over whether or not we will absorb other people's energy in this center is to strengthen the abdominal muscles. This physical strength brings with it emotional strength. The navel center is also the center of creativity. When we consciously choose whose energy to absorb and learn to release, through the use of exercise and visualization, energy that we have absorbed unconsciously, we gain clear access to our creative energy and are able to give it whatever expression (art, writing, dance, etc.) that we choose.

The solar plexus chakra, located just below the sternum, has to do with controlling and working with the physical body. This center is related to our will to grow, to open, to achieve ourselves. We can carry a lot of old judgements and fears in this center. Working to open it helps to clear out these judgements and fears and gives us a greater sense of courage and peace. Working to clear and strengthen the solar plexus chakra, we find ways to create and maintain a balance within ourselves.

The navel and solar plexus chakras are called the "hara" in Japanese, a word meaning belly strength. In the martial arts, many of which particularly emphasize the strengthening of these chakras, the use of sound (counting aloud or making other sounds while exercising) is encouraged. Making sounds causes the abdominal muscles to contract slightly and this helps to strengthen them. When the hara is developed we live life from an organized center, with purpose and direction.

The heart chakra, located in the center of the chest, is the point of integration of body and being. In opening the heart center we learn to give and receive love for ourselves and others. The heart is the center of compassion. When we connect with people from the heart center there is an openness, a spaciousness in the relationship which allows the other to be. There is no clinging or attachment, no limiting or addictive patterns of relationship. The open heart integrates the wisdom of the Earth and the body with the wisdom of the higher being.

The throat chakra, located deep within the throat in the area near the thyroid gland and the ears, is the center of sound. When we open the throat chakra we are able to actualize ourselves through the power of vibration. The throat chakra has to do with communication, our ability to receive our own information (to hear our own inner voice) and to communicate with others.

The chakra known as the "third eye" is located between the eyebrows in the center of the forehead. This is the center of inner sight. It is the place where we receive visions and is the integration point for what we call the conscious and the unconscious.

When the third eye is opened we have conscious access to a deeper wisdom.

The crown chakra is located at the top of the head, at the posterior fontanel, and is known as the spiritual center. This is the place where the light of the heavens, of the universe, enters our body. It is the center of pure knowing. Here we have the wisdom of all lives.

The "Earth and Sky II" meditation helps to open the chakras. When we have the *intention* of opening, and then we work with visualization to open the chakras, they will open. The physical exercises which follow this meditation will also help to open the chakras as will the energy of sound.

> Imagine yourself standing on a beautiful spot upon the Earth. Stand very relaxed, arms hanging easily at your sides, eyes looking straight ahead, feet planted firmly on the Earth. Imagine a huge rock deep in the heart of the Earth. Imagine its vivid colors — rich, earthy colors: reds, oranges, yellows, browns, greens. Imagine these colors as vividly as possible. Imagine energy vibrating from the rock. See it as waves of light. Feel it as a gentle pulse, like a heartbeat, the heartbeat of the Earth.
>
> Now, focus on your breathing and, as you inhale, imagine that you are inhaling the waves of light that are spiraling upward from this rock in the heart of the Earth. Feel the pulse of the Earth. It is very subtle, yet very powerful. Feel the waves of energy from the Earth traveling up and touching the soles of your feet. Feel the energy of the Earth touching the soles of your feet. As you inhale, imagine the energy of the Earth moving through your feet and traveling up through your ankles, calves, knees and thighs. Take your time and draw in the Earth energy with every inhalation, allowing it to travel through your feet and legs, up into your pelvis. Feel its warmth as it fills your pelvis. Sense the energy of the Earth flowing through your hips. Now it enters your spine. Imagine your spine opening, breathing, extending like a long root down into the Earth, to receive the energy of the Earth.
>
> Breathe deeply and feel the Earth energy — those rich, deep, vibrant, pulsing colors — fill your spine. Imagine this energy flowing into your sacrum at the base of your spine. Feel the Earth energy fill your root chakra, the energy center at the base of your spine. Continue to breathe very slowly and deeply and, as you inhale, draw in the Earth energy. As you exhale, feel this energy move up your spine. Inhale and feel the energy moving along your spine, traveling slowly upward and filling your navel chakra. Feel yourself firmly rooted in the Earth as the

Earth energy flows into your navel chakra and continues to flow upward through your body. Now, feel the energy as it fills your solar plexus, the space a few inches above your navel. Feel the warmth as that energy center fills with Earth light. Breathe deeply and draw the energy further up into your body. Feel the energy flow into your heart. Allow the energy to expand, to fill your heart, and to continue to flow upward, spiraling up into your throat center. Feel the energy of the Earth filling your throat chakra.

As you continue to breathe, draw the Earth energy up into your head. Allow it to flow into your third eye, the space between your eyebrows. Feel the Earth energy light up your third eye. Breathe in, and feel the warmth as the energy of the Earth flows higher still, up into the crown chakra, at the top of your head. Imagine a small opening there, through which the Earth energy can flow up and out and arc back down, flowing back into the Earth.

Become aware of the full circle — Earth energy spiraling up through you and returning to the Earth. As the energy flows out the top of your head, it washes down the front, back and sides of your body so that you are surrounded by Earth energy. Allow yourself to really feel or imagine your connection to the Earth. Your spine is a long root, extending deep into the Earth. You are firmly connected to the Earth. Breathe in and receive the energy of the Earth.

Now, imagine the sky energy as a warm golden sun above your head and, as you inhale, feel this energy pouring down upon you. Feel it enter your body through the opening in the crown chakra. Feel the warmth of the golden light of the sun as it infuses your body and travels downward, filling each energy center in turn. Feel, sense, or imagine this energy flowing into your third eye. Inhale, and allow the sky energy to flow downward into your throat chakra. As you continue to inhale, the sky energy is spiraling downward, filling your body. It is moving into your heart. Feel your heart opening, feel more space as you fill with sky energy. The sky energy flows downward now into your solar plexus and further down into your navel center and into the base of your spine. Now it flows through your pelvis and hips, down through your legs and enters your feet. The sky energy flows through the soles of your feet, into the Earth. Sense the full circle of sky energy.

You are surrounded by and bathed in the energy of the Earth and of the sky. Feel the safety, the warmth and the nourishment as you are fed by Earth and sky. Know that you are upon this Earth and you are nourished and sustained by the Earth. The wisdom of your being, beyond time and space, fills your body as the warm golden light from the sky fills you. Earth and sky, Earth and sky. You are one with the Earth and sky.

Exercises to Open the Body

Dancer-healer, Bonnie Novakov-Lawlor, has developed an excellent series of physical exercises based on the flow of Earth and sky energy and its manifestation in the body. Bonnie has kindly allowed me to include these exercises in *The Inner Dance*.[5] They work hand in hand with the visualization exercises. As you are doing the physical movements, you are to imagine yourself connecting to the energy of both Earth and sky. The primary objective of these exercises is to develop a strong feeling awareness of the body and of the body's alignment. These exercises are only a foundation. There are many more exercises that could be included in a daily physical routine, but the principles of alignment upon which this series is based and the way of working carefully with breath, awareness and softening described here are applicable to any exercise program.

There are several images used throughout the discussion of body work and throughout the visualizations as well. The first is "to ground." To ground means to feel the body weight reaching down into and connecting with the Earth. The second is "to soften." This means to relax, to imagine the breath moving through a particular area so that the body part is opening, stretching and becoming longer. A third image is that of keeping an area of the body "open and breathing." By this, I mean that you are to imagine that area of the body, for example, the base of the spine, with breath flowing through it. Imagining the breath flowing freely through the base of the spine aids in keeping the spine correctly aligned. It creates a feeling of space rather than the feeling of compression we often experience. Another image is that of "working" a body part. To work the abdominals, for example, means to activate those muscles and feel them lengthening. This is different than simply tightening them, which can cause gripping. It is helpful to imagine the abdominal muscles lifting up and emptying into the back.

The soul's wisdom, in order to be fully actualized, needs to be grounded in the physical body yet many people who are drawn to psychic and spiritual work are unaware of the need for grounding. A strong, stable base of support is necessary so that we can draw upon the higher vibrations. The higher vibrations are actually an electrical current, so, if we do not adequately prepare the nervous system and the physical body, these vibrations can cause us to experience burn-out, just as when lightning strikes something that is not grounded it causes a fire. As the physical body becomes stronger, we lessen our need to brace ourselves, to protect ourselves against something or to attach ourselves to something, so we have greater movement and flexibility.

We want to develop a strong base of support in the lower body, allowing gravity and the weight of the body to serve us, making sure that the appropriate muscles work to support the spine and ribs so that the heart can open. A strong physical support is developed when the feet, ankles, legs and abdominal muscles become strong and flexible. If the muscles in the lower part of the body are weak, the upper body compensates with tension. In attempting to maintain our stance, we develop a collapsed chest, tense and hunched-over shoulders and stiff necks. A collapsed chest and weak base can also come from psychic and emotional pain or *vice versa*. Whatever the reason, working to correct this alignment will make a change on both levels, giving us greater physical and emotional security. In this ever-changing world we need a strong base. The only real security, as Bonnie explains, "is in our relationship to the Earth. The more deeply we can root ourselves in the Mother (Earth), the more we are able to open to reality."

These exercises pay particular attention to grounding and drawing the Earth energy up through the feet. If you are not able to stand on your feet, you can ground to the Earth energy through the buttocks or bring it directly into the back. You can also ground through your hands or your knees.

In proper alignment there is a natural curve of the spine. Without correct and adequate muscle support, the spinal column collapses and the curve is exaggerated, causing pain, injury or disease. "In dance," Bonnie explains, "we unfold the body between two points, the coccyx and the sternum. This line from coccyx to sternum gives the full vertical alignment."

The exercises given here focus on developing and sensing this alignment in each posture through attention to deep, full breathing, openness and position of the feet, lengthening of the waist through the gentle working of the abdominal muscles (contracting slightly without gripping), openness of the ribs, and relaxation of the hips, shoulders and neck. While doing the exercises, be aware of the difference between gently working the muscles, which is most beneficial, and gripping, which is not. It is important to allow the muscles to support the spine without holding tightly. The entire body is one. When one part changes and lets go, another part will need to be readjusted. We continually work with the total relationship. These exercises are a process of carefully sensing, and moving towards, rather than achieving, a set form. Never work past your true level of openness for, in doing so, you may throw something out of alignment. Allow the stretches to help you find the edge where you need to breathe deeply and let go in order to achieve more space and a deeper relationship to the body.

Bonnie suggests that you do sounding during the exercises. In sounding, the breath is maintained and the throat chakra stays open. If we can stay open in the throat chakra, the energy will flow in and out in a circular motion and all our movements will be more fluid. Sounding can be accomplished by counting while stretching. Make the voice real, as pleasing and flowing as possible, so that the throat doesn't tense. Feel the vibration in the body and, as you lower your focus to your abdominals, your voice will deepen and clear.

The final posture depends on the beginning posture, so the exercises begin and end with standing. Standing is a constant act of balancing, reorganizing and readjusting. The description of the standing posture is very detailed in order to help you develop an awareness of the vertical alignment of the body and be aware of this vertical in every position.

The muscles are memory banks, holding within them all the

experiences of the body. Doing these exercises may "light up" some issues for you, perhaps bringing painful memories to your awareness and allowing you to release them. So, be sure to do these exercises gently and with full awareness. If painful memories do surface, you may want to enlist the aid of a therapist or healer or someone skilled in body work to help with the process of release.

In doing this work, we first imagine what the body can do and, gradually, the body begins to do it. The body has its own wisdom. Practice the exercises even when you are not absolutely sure of a position. As you practice, your body will give you feedback. The body wants to move and stretch. Working with these exercises will help you to find your correct alignment; you are not expected to have it when you are just starting out. Read all of the exercises through several times before attempting them. And, each time, before beginning to do them, take a few minutes to do the "Earth and Sky" meditation. Remember that you are a conduit for energy, that energy is flowing through you. At the same time you are reaching down into the Earth you are also reaching up into the sky.

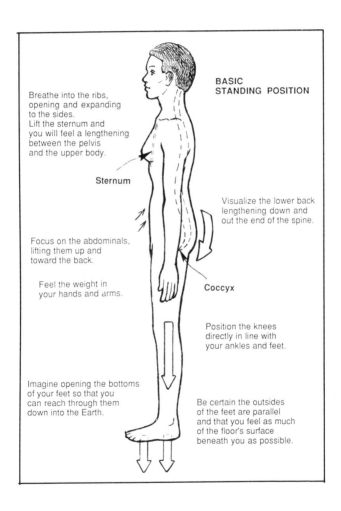

Breathe into the ribs,
opening and expanding
to the sides.
Lift the sternum and
you will feel a lengthening
between the pelvis
and the upper body.

Sternum

**BASIC
STANDING POSITION**

Visualize the lower back
lengthening down and
out the end of the spine.

Focus on the abdominals,
lifting them up and
toward the back.

Feel the weight in
your hands and arms.

Coccyx

Position the knees
directly in line with
your ankles and feet.

Imagine opening the bottoms
of your feet so that you
can reach through them
down into the Earth.

Be certain the outsides
of the feet are parallel
and that you feel as much
of the floor's surface
beneath you as possible.

Warm-up Sequence I

Standing —

Begin by directing your attention to your feet, making certain the outsides of your feet are parallel to each other and that your feet are fully on the floor so that you can feel as much of the floor's surface beneath you as possible. Sense, feel, or imagine the Earth's energy through the points in the ball of your foot on either side of the metatarsal arch and on either side of the heel. It is the awareness of the Earth's energy that will ground you. Exert a gentle pull upward through the abdominals. Take the weight forward into the balls of the feet so that the heels are free. Then stretch the heels back down to the floor in as smooth a movement as possible. This begins to give full length to the legs and to organize the center of the body's weight properly in the pelvis and in the feet. Imagine opening the bottoms of your feet so that you can reach through them, down into the Earth. Again focus on the abdominals, lifting them up and toward the back. Visualizing the lower back lengthening down and out the end of the spine will bring the pelvis into position. (We are working for this pelvic position in all postures.)

Breathe into the ribs, allow them to open and expand out to the sides. Lift gently in the sternum (upper breast bone). As you breathe into this area, feel a lengthening through the waist that begins to occur between the pelvis and the upper body. Maintain this gentle lift through the sternum and continue to reach into the Earth through the feet. Breathe into the shoulders and feel them relax... Allow their weight to pour down the chest, back and outside of your arms. Feel the weight in your arms and hands as they hang relaxed at your sides. Now, focus your attention on positioning the knees so that they are directly in line with your ankles and feet. You will feel your buttocks respond by contracting gently towards each other.

Again feel that the base of the spine is open, your breath

flowing through it. Check again to see that your hands still feel heavy. Allow the back of your neck to stretch gently upward, your head to rest easily on your neck and your eyes to be open and look ahead. See the room you are in. Feel the lift in your sternum. Center your consciousness in your pelvis and breathe deeply and slowly. Be aware of your legs reaching down into your feet and down into the Earth.

This is the basic position. All the other exercises given here are designed to strengthen and bring awareness to this way of being in the body.

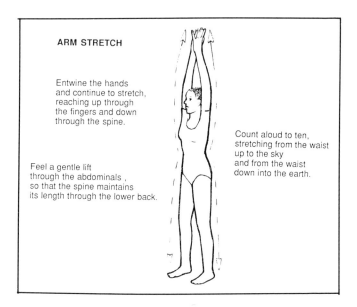

ARM STRETCH

Entwine the hands
and continue to stretch,
reaching up through
the fingers and down
through the spine.

Feel a gentle lift
through the abdominals ,
so that the spine maintains
its length through the lower back.

Count aloud to ten,
stretching from the waist
up to the sky
and from the waist
down into the earth.

Arm stretch —

Stand in the basic posture and, as for all the standing exercises, feel a gentle lift through the abdominals. Stretch the arms out very far from the sides of the body. Keep the fingers open and extend the elbows and wrists fully, feeling the stretch through the arms, hands and ribs. Continue stretching the arms out and up until they are overhead. Entwine the hands and continue to stretch, reaching up through the fingers and down through the feet. Count aloud to ten, stretching from the waist up to the sky and from the waist down into the Earth. As the stretch continues, the abdominals need to work more strongly so that the spine maintains its length through the lower back.

Knee Bends —

From the arm stretch, release your hands and drop over, bending your knees. Fold your spine over, relax your neck so that your head is heavy and hanging down. Feel the weight in your feet and bend your knees a little more. With the spine still folded and the head remaining down, straighten the knees so that the sit bones are reaching up to the sky. When the legs are extended as much as possible, take a deep breath and imagine exhaling through your hip joints so that they release even more and the backs of the thighs begin to release as well. The head will release, falling more toward the floor. Breathe into and work with the stretch for ten counts. Bend the knees again. Feel the support system of the legs and the feet and the support of the Earth beneath them. Keep the spine folded over and the head down. Stretch your arms behind your back, clasping your hands, keeping the thumbs up. Reach out through the hands and down and out through the feet so that the pelvis and chest open. Your chest will move closer to your thighs. Drop your hands and feel the total weight of the arms and hands as they hang from the shoulders. Work to keep the chest as close to the thighs as possible while keeping the head down, and the shoulders and neck relaxed. Breathe into the stretch. Feel the support coming up through the feet as you again straighten the legs and push the sit bones up into the sky. When your head and neck are fully relaxed, you will feel like you are upside down. Breathe into the stretch for ten counts. Bend at the knees again and relax. As you roll up, feel the coccyx. Bring it under as though you had a tail between your legs and were pulling it down and forward. The knees and spine unfold simultaneously. All movement is coming from the navel center. As you straighten, bring your consciousness directly into the lift of the sternum. This will allow your shoulders to drop and you will be in the full standing position. Breathe.

This warm-up sequence can be done several times quickly once you have learned it.

KNEE BENDS

When the legs are extended as much as possible, take a deep breath and imagine exhaling through your hip joints. Breathe into and work with the stretch for ten counts.

Relax your neck so that your head is heavy and hanging down.

Keep your spine folded over and the head down, clasping the hands behind the back, keeping the thumbs up. Reach out through the hands and down and through the feet, so that the pelvis and chest open.

The Chakras in Relation to the Physical Exercises

Root chakra — Focusing on the coccyx brings energy into the root chakra and helps to ground. Rolling up and dropping down from the base of the spine with the floor of the pelvis open (that is, with relaxed genitals, perineum and anus) opens and energizes the root chakra.

Navel chakra — Lifting the abdominal muscles opens and strengthens all the lower chakras, especially the navel chakra.

Solar Plexus Chakra — Working to expand the ribs opens the solar plexus and allows more energy to circulate throughout the entire body.

Heart chakra — Lifting the sternum and allowing the shoulders to drop opens the heart chakra. Grounding the lower body and stretching out the vertical activates the ribs and the abdominals, allowing the heart chakra to open and all the chakras to receive more energy. The arm stretches given here also help to open the heart.

Throat chakra — Lifting the sternum and allowing the shoulders to drop gives space to the throat chakra. Sounding keeps the throat chakra open.

Third eye chakra — Supporting the torso from the base and lifting the sternum relaxes the neck and head and gives proper support so that the third eye can open. Keeping the neck loose keeps the third eye open. When the body is well grounded there is less clutter around the third eye so, rather than thinking all the time, one is being.

Crown chakra — Supporting from underneath and establishing a strong vertical allows the crown chakra to open.

Warm-up Sequence II

Warm-up Sequence II follows Warm-up Sequence I. It can also be done several times quickly once you have learned it.

Standing Side Stretch —

Stand with your feet parallel and three feet apart, feeling that they are well planted in the Earth. The knees are in line with the ankles, the abdominals are contracted slightly, the back is long and the sternum is lifting gently. Keep the pelvis square to the front and drop the spine to the side, feeling the curve of the spine. Let the head and neck be part of the curve. Keep the hips facing forward and the weight centered evenly on both feet. Feel the weight of the head and chest, and allow it to deepen the stretch. Feel the supporting strength of the legs, feet and pelvis. Increase the stretch by lifting the opposite arm up and stretching it toward the sky. The other arm is reaching down into the Earth, sliding down along the outside of the leg. Think of stretching the arm out of the chest rather than out of the shoulders. Use the abdominals to maintain the position of the pelvis. Breathe into the stretch for ten counts. Then repeat the stretch on the other side of your body.

Neck Stretch —

Still standing with the feet about three feet apart, with attention to grounding and alignment, stretch the head to the right, and return it to center. Stretch the head forward and then to center. Left and center. Back and center. Pay attention to the weight of the head and the neck. Feel the weight of the jaw. Make the jaw tight and feel how it tightens the whole body. Now relax the jaw. Work with the jaw relaxed. This stretch places less stress on the neck vertebrae than a full head roll. Do this stretch several times.

STANDING SIDE STRETCH

Use the abdominals to maintain
the pelvis square to the front
and keep the weight evenly
distributed between the legs.

Lift the opposite arm out of the
chest rather than the shoulder,
and reach toward the sky.
The arm along the leg reaches
down into the Earth.

Breathe into the stretch
for ten counts.

NECK STRETCH

Maintain your stance with feet apart and attention to grounding and alignment.

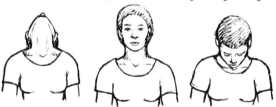

Elongate the neck front and back, so it is not constricted.
Allow the weight of the head and jaw to help with this stretch.
Release unnecessary tension in the face and jaw.

Knee Bends —

Fold the spine over and bend the knees so that they are positioned directly over the ankles. Place your elbows inside your knees, and your hands on the floor. Relax into the stretch. With your knees bent, feel the weight of the body in the feet and in the arms. Imagine exhaling through the hip joints. Keep breathing and work the chest close to the thighs. Continue the stretch for a count of ten. Straighten the knees while keeping the spine and head down. Feel the sit bones reaching up into he sky. When you can no longer extend the stretch, take a deep breath and imagine exhaling through the hips. Relax your shoulders and arms completely. Continue to feel the stretch. Breathe and feel your entire body softening for a count of ten. Bend your knees and, focusing on the coccyx and sternum, roll up into a standing position. Unfold your knees and your spine simultaneously.

Floor Exercises

Complete Breathing —

Lie on your back with your legs slightly apart, your knees bent and your feet flat on the floor. Feel the floor. Keep your arms relaxed at your sides. Make sure the small of your back is touching the floor. Relax your shoulders.

Inhale slowly and evenly into the sacrum, slightly increasing the pressure from the sacrum toward the floor by using the breath, not pushing down with the muscles. The abdomen extends slightly and the breath moves up through the diaphragm, into the sides of the ribs and into the collar bones. With practice, the breath can also move up into the roof of the mouth. Exhale by gently contracting the abdomen and using those muscles to push the breath up through the body and out through the nose, as if you were squeezing a tube of toothpaste. The ribs stay open and the spine remains elongated. The abdominal muscles are always working gently so that there is no ballooning of the abdomen during the inhalation. Work towards breathing in a fluid, continuous rhythm. The breath rolls like a wave through the body.

Begin slowly, doing only a few complete breaths and increase gradually each day.

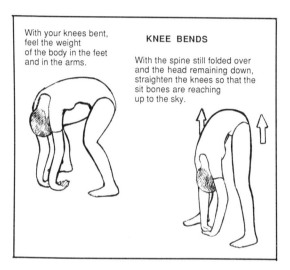

With your knees bent, feel the weight of the body in the feet and in the arms.

KNEE BENDS

With the spine still folded over and the head remaining down, straighten the knees so that the sit bones are reaching up to the sky.

COMPLETE BREATHING

Inhale slowly and evenly into the sacrum, using the breath to press the sacrum into the floor. The abdomen will extend slightly and the breath will move up through the ribs and into the collar bones.

Exhale by gently contracting the abdomen and pushing the breath up though the body and out through the nose. Keep the ribs open and elongate the spine.

Abdominal Exercises —

Lie on your back with your knees bent and arms at your sides. Press the small of your back gently against the floor. Check the position of the knees to be sure they are not rolling in but are aligned with your feet, which are parallel. Keep the hips squared. Imagine emptying the belly into the back so that the belly becomes soft and the abdominals are pulled in and up. Keep your feet firmly on the floor and, with your hands pulling against your inner thighs, raise your neck and shoulders off the floor. Now release the hands and maintain the position. Begin by making very small, smooth reaches (one to one and a half inches) stretching your arms and fingers through your legs. Focus your consciousness in the abdomen. Count aloud from one to twenty. Rest when you need to, gradually working toward one hundred reaches. The movements should be very small and smooth. If there is jerking, it means the shoulders are tensing. Release the shoulders and refocus the consciousness. You will feel the movement in the upper abdomen under the ribs at first but, eventually, you will feel it more and more deeply in the lower abdomen.

Transverse Abdominals —

Lie in the same position as above. Make sure the hips are squared. Feel the feet firmly on the ground. Use the hands on the inner thighs to pull the neck and shoulders off the floor. The goal is not to get so far off the ground but to make a smooth curve of the upper body and neck and to work from the abdominals. Release the hands. Make a shallow rotation to one side of the body, so that the inside corner of the shoulder can stretch toward the opposite knee. Make small reaches with the hands. Count aloud from one to twenty. Return to the starting position, rest, and bring your focus into the lower pelvis. Then begin the exercise again on the other side.

ABDOMINAL EXERCISES

Keep your feet firmly planted and with your hands on your inner thighs, pull to raise your neck and shoulders off the ground.
Then release the hands and maintain the position.

Make small smooth reaches
stretching hands and fingers through the legs.
Focus your attention in your abdomen and count to twenty.

TRANSVERSE ABDOMINALS

Make a smooth curve in the upper body and neck
and work from the abdominals
.to create the stretch.

Make a shallow rotation
to one side, so that
the inside of the shoulder
reaches toward the opposite knee.

Engaging the Psoas Muscles and
Stretching the Feet —

This is an exploratory, sensing exercise to see how the leg is lifted from the abdomen as well as to develop strength and stretch. To gain full strength and alignment, it is important to feel how the legs are connected to the torso by the psoas muscle, which extends from the inner thigh up through the abdomen and into the back. The objective here is to work the abdominals, keeping the leg long.

Lie on your back with one knee bent to give support to the body and the other leg extended. The hips are squared, the small of the back is pressed into the floor. The head is raised slightly, the hands are clasped behind the neck with the elbows extending outward. Using the abdominal muscles, lift your leg slightly and stretch out your foot and ankle, vigorously reaching through the arch and toes as though you are wrapping the bottom of the foot around a golden ball. Now, flex the foot and ankle, and stretch open the foot by making as much width as possible between the bones in the metatarsal arch. Do fifteen tiny leg lifts and complete the exercise with five long lifts. Reach from the belly to lift the leg. The small of the back will move more solidly against the floor. Your objective is to lengthen the leg and foot, not to raise the leg as high as possible. Send your energy out through the toes while feeling the abdominals activate and lengthen.

PSOAS MUSCLES and FOOT STRETCH

Clasp the hands behind the head, with the elbows extended outward.

Align the hips evenly and press the small of the back gently to the floor.

Lift the extended leg slightly and stretch out of the foot and ankle.

Reach through the arch and toes as though you are wrapping the bottom of the foot around a golden ball.

Spinal Rotation —

Lie on your back with your knees bent. Keep the hips squared, the small of the back on the floor, the shoulders relaxed. Reaching out with the arms, extend them perpendicular to the spine. Look at your arms to check position. Stretch the hands and fingers vigorously. Feel an opening through the chest. Think of reaching with the palms and fingers all the way out from the center of the chest. You should feel this through the arm and armpit as well as in your hands, fingers and chest. Now, extend one leg with the foot flexed, while keeping the other leg bent. Moving strongly from the abdomen so that the back and spine maintain their length, reach across the body with the extended leg. The bent knee will automatically fall to the floor. Work to keep the opposite hand and arm reaching. Continue the stretch for a count of ten. Then release and do the stretch with the other leg extended. Roll onto your back and draw both knees up to your chest. Breathe into your hip joints and let your knees drop toward your chest. Then release.

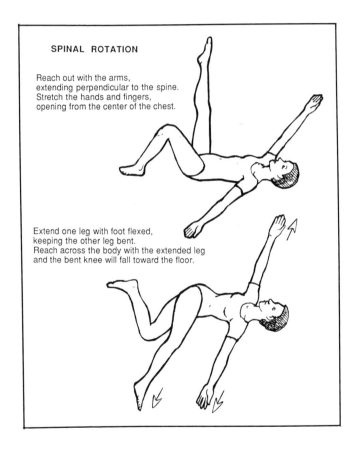

SPINAL ROTATION

Reach out with the arms,
extending perpendicular to the spine.
Stretch the hands and fingers,
opening from the center of the chest.

Extend one leg with foot flexed,
keeping the other leg bent.
Reach across the body with the extended leg
and the bent knee will fall toward the floor.

Child Pose —

Kneel on the floor, knees together, sitting on your heels with the tops of your feet flat on the floor. Slowly bend forward, sliding your arms and hands, palms flat, straight out in front of your body until your back is rounded and your chest touches your legs. Feel the coccyx come forward. Feel the hips release. Allow the forehead to drop to the floor and walk the fingers out as far as possible. Breathe and soften. Raise your head and upper back so that your eyes are looking straight ahead

Be sure to maintain the position of your hips and fingers. Breathe. Then roll back up until you are standing on your knees.

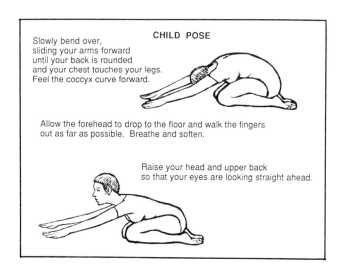

CHILD POSE

Slowly bend over, sliding your arms forward until your back is rounded and your chest touches your legs. Feel the coccyx curve forward.

Allow the forehead to drop to the floor and walk the fingers out as far as possible. Breathe and soften.

Raise your head and upper back so that your eyes are looking straight ahead.

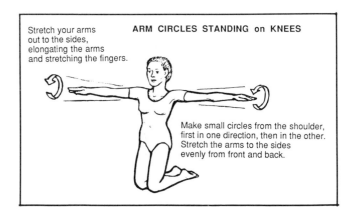

Stretch your arms out to the sides, elongating the arms and stretching the fingers.

ARM CIRCLES STANDING on KNEES

Make small circles from the shoulder, first in one direction, then in the other. Stretch the arms to the sides evenly from front and back.

Arm Circles Standing on Knees —

Taking the weight fully on the knees, lift the abdomen and sternum and feel the coccyx reach down and push slightly forward. You will feel this stretch in the backs of the thighs, an important group of muscles in the standing position as well as in this position. Stretch your arms out to the sides, making them very long and working the fingers. Make small circles from the shoulder, first in one direction, then in the other. Be careful not to take your arms behind you as this will close the back. The arms should stretch to the sides evenly from front and back. Rest.

Back and Thigh Stretch on Knees —

Stand on your knees and extend your arms out to the sides. Inhale. As you exhale, lean back in one piece from the knees. Reach forward and up with the arms. Look up toward the sky. As you return to the vertical, again in one piece, let your arms return to your sides. Inhale. Again, exhale as you lean back from the knees, arms and eyes reaching up and forward. Your abdominals and the backs of your legs are working hard. Be careful to take this movement only as far as you feel comfortable because it also stretches the muscles around the knees which, for many people, are a weak point. Imagine that there is an elastic string that stretches but never breaks between your sternum and heaven, and allow yourself to feel the emotional aspect of reaching with your heart to the sky. Now, lie on your side with your bottom arm extended under your head. Your upper arm can steady your body, with the elbow bent and the palm on the floor in front of your chest. Align the body so that it is directly perpendicular to the floor. The upper knee is bent and rests on the floor. Extend and stretch the lower leg, reaching through the big toe. Slowly lift this leg ten times while strongly lifting the abdominals into your back. Feel the inside surface of the ankle reaching to the sky. Your toes are pointed down. Your foot and leg will feel further forward than you expect when the abdominals are working properly and the spine is long. Repeat the exercise on the other side.

Outside Leg Lift —

Lie on your side with your lower leg well bent. Extend the upper leg with the foot flexed, as closely perpendicular to the torso as possible. Gently rotate the hip back so that the leg and foot are not turned in. Stretch deeply into the heel and let the energy out through the toes. Feel the connection of the toes with the crown of the head. Lift the upper leg, in small lifts, ten times. Your leg should feel heavy. Feel the connection between the weight of your

BACK and THIGH STRETCH on KNEES

As you exhale, lean back
in one piece from the knees.
Reach forward and up with the arms.
Look up towards the sky.
Feel the emotional aspect
of reaching with your heart to the sky.

As you return to the vertical,
again in one piece,
let your arms return to your sides.

OUTSIDE LEG LIFT

Stretch deeply into the raised heel
and let the energy out through the toes.
Put the leg down and lift it
with the hip, without using
the abdominals.

foot and your abdominals.

Put the leg down and lift it with the hip, without using
the abdominals, and feel the lightness. Then relax the hip.
Feel the weight of the leg and foot and work to lift from
the abdominals. Relax. Lie on the other side and repeat
the exercise with the other leg.

The Serpent —

Lie flat on the floor, face down, with your forehead touching the floor. Start by placing your palms next to your shoulders. Stretch your legs, feet and toes vigorously while pressing the insides of your legs together. Your kneecaps face straight down so that the buttocks contract toward each other and the abdominals lift up and into the back, as in the standing position. Inhale deeply through the abdomen, ribs and neck and, as you exhale, maintain the length in your lower pelvis and legs. Push your hands against the ground to lift your head and chest. Breathe deeply, feel your breath helping you relax into the position. Think of lengthening vigorously through the abdominals into the back. It is here, in the lower abdominals, that you want to feel the stretch. There should be no crunching in the small of the back. Think of sending energy out through the feet and toes and through the hands and fingers. This will help to maintain length and protect the back. Again, feel your breath helping you to relax into the position. As you breathe, you should feel your ribs opening and your abdominals working. Release any tension in your shoulders, letting them fall down at the same time as you are lengthening your neck and pulling your head up. Breathe. The aim here is not so much to lift up high in the chest as to lengthen your torso from the abdomen. Relax. Roll over and bring your knees up to your chest.

If The Serpent exercise causes strain on the small of the back, work with your legs slightly apart, bent at the knees, so that the shins are perpendicular to the ground and the arms are stretched down by the sides. Work to draw the insides of the legs together, once you have lifted your head, chest and knees off the ground.

The Plough —

Lie on your back with your legs together. Pull your belly gently into your back so that the abdominals are acti-

THE SERPENT

Think of lengthening the abdominals and
send the energy through the feet and toes
and through the hands and fingers,
pressing the insides of the legs together.

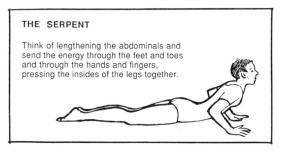

THE PLOUGH

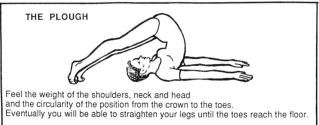

Feel the weight of the shoulders, neck and head
and the circularity of the position from the crown to the toes.
Eventually you will be able to straighten your legs until the toes reach the floor.

vated. Folding your knees toward your chest, lift the hips
and legs up and over your head. You may use your hands
to support your waist as your legs are going over. Release
any tension in the hips. Breathe deeply so that the knees
come closer to your ears. Feel the weight of your neck,
head and shoulders. Allow them to sink and lengthen into
the floor and allow energy to extend out through the top
of your head. Breathe deeply. Gently lift your sternum
toward your chin. Your abdominals are working softly.
Gently straighten your legs and release your hands from
your waist, letting them lie flat on the floor with the palms
down. Again, feel the circularity of the position from toes
to crown. Breathe deeply and experience the feeling this
exercise creates in your body. With practice, you will eventually be able to straighten your legs until your toes reach
the floor.

Now, slowly and gently roll down, feeling each ver-
tebra as it touches the floor.

Seated Side Stretch —

Sit on the floor with one leg extended on the diagonal and the other leg bent, with the heel close to the floor of the pelvis. Feel the sit bones reaching into the Earth. Keep the buttocks on the floor with your weight balanced evenly between them. Your hips should be facing forward. Rotate your upper torso so that the shoulder and side ribs are lined up with the extended leg. While keeping the abdominals lifted and feeling the legs stretching, bring the arm nearest the extended leg out and along the inside of the leg. Bend at the elbow and grasp under the calf or ankle (depending on which is more comfortable for you) and breathe into the stretch. Now, raise the other arm up toward the sky. Continue to reach out with the long arm, stretching the spine toward the extended foot, using the hand under your calf or ankle to help. Your abdominals should be working to help keep the pelvis and sit bones in line with each other. Hold for a count of ten, breathing deeply and slowly and feeling the stretch. Release, slowly returning your torso to an upright position. Now do this stretch on the other side.

Open Leg Stretch —

Open both legs to the diagonals. Lift your body on your hands and slide your pelvis forward a few more inches. Reach into the Earth with your sit bones and lengthen your legs and feet, sending energy out through the toes. Gently roll the knees so that the kneecaps face the sky. This will stretch and open the hips. Breathe into the floor of the pelvis, into your ribs and sternum. Now release the sit bones and reach from your pelvis toward the floor. Work to keep your kneecaps facing skyward. Relax your shoulders. They do not need to work at all. The movement comes from the pelvis. Direct your breath into any areas where you feel tension and relax. Hold for a count of ten and slowly return to the vertical. Breathe deeply and rotate your torso toward your right leg and, reaching

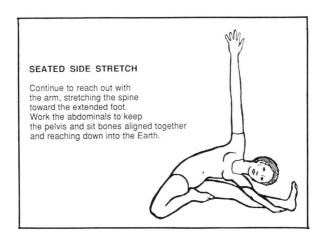

SEATED SIDE STRETCH

Continue to reach out with
the arm, stretching the spine
toward the extended foot.
Work the abdominals to keep
the pelvis and sit bones aligned together
and reaching down into the Earth.

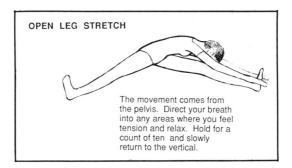

OPEN LEG STRETCH

The movement comes from
the pelvis. Direct your breath
into any areas where you feel
tension and relax. Hold for a
count of ten and slowly
return to the vertical.

from the pelvis, stretch your torso over this leg. Breathe deeply, feel the stretch and hold for a count of ten. Release, slowly returning to the vertical. Breathe deeply and stretch over your left leg. Hold for a count of ten and again return to the vertical.

Rocking Release —

Get on your hands and knees and enthusiastically rock your body back and forth like a little child attempting to crawl. Let the movement be large and playful. This movement provides a release on a very deep level.

Standing Dog Stretch —

Keeping your hands on the floor, come up onto your feet for a last stretch. Make your legs long and point your sit bones up toward the sky. Keep your abdominals working and your shoulders relaxed. Increase this stretch by extending your arms forward, keeping the palms flat on the floor. Bend your knees, bring your hands close to your body and, straightening your knees, roll up into the standing position, again feeling the coccyx come forward and a lift up through the sternum.

STANDING DOG STRETCH

Make your legs long and point your sit bones up toward the sky. Keep your abdominals working and your shoulders relaxed.

Walking —

Using the abdominals and the backs of the legs for support, push up onto the balls of the feet and then back down so that the feet are flat on the floor. Do this slowly, ten times. The insides of the ankles and legs should be reaching strongly for each other. Now walk briskly around the space in which you have been exercising. Continue to be aware of your deep and relaxed breathing. Be aware of the lengthening in your lower back and the feeling of the coccyx pushing slightly forward. Feel your abdominals working and feel the lift in your sternum so that your torso feels like a nice long vertical. Relax your shoulders with a downward pull and let your arms swing naturally at your sides. Allow your head to gently float upward and keep your eyes focused and alert. Imagine cutting though the air with your sternum as you move gracefully through the space, breathing easily. Feel your feet, legs and abdominals strongly supporting you and keeping you deeply connected with the Earth. Keep breathing.

IV
Exploration

We open ourselves like the air, and the world flows through us
like the wind.... We have no boundaries — we are all we experience,
know, feel — all of which interacts with everything,
making us of the entire earth. Through the old ways,
we are in harmony with all circumstances — the correct and harmonious
course of action is always to be found in us if we are
in touch with ourselves.

—Gayle High Pine

Opening the self is a process that begins in silence as we spend time observing and exploring our breathing, the sensations and feelings in our bodies, the thoughts and images in our minds. Our experiences in life may have been such that, without knowing it, we have chosen to shut down. We may not even be aware of our feelings or of the constant chatter that goes on in our minds. Our mental images may be confused, hazy or frightening. We may get flashes of insight and not trust them. When we attempt to observe the breath, we may not be able to find it. Fear and tension may be blocking sensation in our bodies. A friend once told me a story about a woman, who, upon hearing her heartbeat for the first time, thought something was wrong and consulted a doctor. This story may be extreme but it illustrates the fear we can encounter when we begin to truly explore the self.

We all have secrets — some deep pain or humiliation we have been hiding from ourselves or from others. To explore the mind is to be a pioneer investigating uncharted territory. Our journeys thus far have carried us far outside of ourselves. The mind is the last frontier. We must be courageous if we are to embark upon this awakening. In seeking out the most distant reaches of the mind, the hidden corners of pain, greed, anger and sorrow are exposed. We must overcome our restlessness, our laziness and the fear that separates us from knowing the truth of our being. There are so many gaps in our knowing and it is these gaps which create all the "isms" that separate us: sexism, racism, ageism, classism. All these gaps are pockets of fear and holding.

The fear that separates us from truth may be self-doubt. We may doubt our ability to cope with the pain hidden in the recesses of our mind. We may feel fear and despair about our survival; it may be a personal fear of rape, robbery or illness or a more global fear of nuclear destruction, pollution, starvation or acid rain. The fear response, regardless of its cause, is an automatic shutting down of our sensitivity and awareness in order to protect ourselves from problems and stress. If we could transcend the tendency to shut down, if we could remain open, we might find, in that open space, new energy, creative perspectives and solutions to many of life's problems.

The answer to any of life's problems, whether as global as the threat of nuclear war, or as personal as coping with the loss of a loved one, begins with awareness. Much of our time is spent in mindless activity. Because we are not in touch with what motivates us, we are pushed and pulled through life by fears and pretenses, by greed, longing and pain. Yet, there are vast reservoirs of love that lie beneath our fears. Hidden behind our pretense is the authenticity of our being. Behind our irresponsibility lies an incredible power to respond. Our denial hides our remarkable ability to be fully present, to inspire others. And, behind our secrets and lies, is the ability to know and speak our own truth. The withholding and the giving up of our power masks our ability to be powerful, clear and purposeful human beings.

Awakening to our own inner dance and to the dance of the universe demands our courage, our willingness to dig beneath the layers of pain and find the hidden treasures. These treasures are our inheritance. Each of us has incredible wealth within us. Each of us has the power to see the beauty and possibility of each moment without prejudice or expectation. Our wealth is an openness of heart, an ability to feel. We can become unafraid of expressing pain or sadness, or of showing uncertainty. The richness of our being is the ability to trust ourselves, to share our particular wisdom and insight.

To sense the deep and continuing connection with all of life, to feel, to respond, to be one with life is a gift that we can accept. It is this gift that allows us to become sensible, sensitive human beings. Awareness brings us from separation into relation. Self knowledge is translated into actions that are "in harmony with all circumstances." As a part of the Earth, we care for the Earth. As a part of each other, we care for each other. What happens to us, happens to our neighbors. What happens to our neighborhoods, happens to our nations. My teacher, Dhyani Ywahoo, has often asked, "What good is it if you can grow corn, if your neighbors are starving?"

The task of exploration is strenuous. It calls for our patience, courage and perseverance. As pioneers of the mind, we go wholeheartedly into the unknown. As we sit and explore who we are, we find that nothing separate, solid or static exists. Who we are, this personal self, is revealed as a changing process of body/mind. In this acknowledgement we become the love, the light, of which this universe is made. "We open ourselves like air, and the world flows through us like the wind."

Exploring Sensations

The exercise, "Exploring Sensations," works with bodily sensations, such as heat, cold, tingling and tightness, as objects of concentration. When we pay close attention to a sensation — breathing, for example — we notice that it is always changing. The secret is this: anything we cling to eventually causes pain. If we held onto the food we ate without the process of elimination, we would become poisoned. If we held onto the breath without exhalation, we would suffocate. But, interestingly enough, before this could happen we would lose consciousness so that the body's natural functioning would interrupt the mind's tendency to cling.

While sitting and observing the body, we may experience tension or pain. We can experiment with two approaches to these sensations — we can learn to breathe through the body part where we are holding pain in order to relax it, or we can change position. Eventually we will have a sense of which approach is most helpful in each moment.

Begin by taking several slow, deep breaths. Now let your breath flow naturally and bring your attention to the sensations in your body. Let your awareness sweep over your body. Does it feel heavy or light? Are you experiencing hot or cold? Is there pain or tension anywhere in your body? Focus clearly on the sensations in your body. Is there tingling or tension? Is there numbness or tickling? Be fully aware of your body. Can you feel the breath, hear the heartbeat? Are you aware of the pulse in any part of your body? Pay very close attention to your body. Is there noise or movement in your stomach? In your intestines? Is there excess energy in your hands, feet, head or any bodily part?

Each time you are aware of any sensation, bring your full attention to that sensation. Explore it deeply. Sit quietly with the sensation. If you feel a desire to move your body, to change your position, do so very slowly, maintaining awareness of each motion.

Now, bring your awareness to each part of your body in turn, beginning with your head. Carefully explore your head. Let your consciousness encircle the outer dimensions of your head and then explore deep within, moving through scalp, bone and tissue, exploring the deep cavities of your head. Breathe in through your nostrils and imagine your breath flowing out through the base of your head.

Bring your awareness into your neck and then your shoulders, exploring them in a very deep and careful way. Notice where there is any soreness or tightness. Breathe through these body parts. Observe carefully and notice all sensations. Notice if there is any difference in sensation before, during, or after the exploration.

Let your awareness travel to your arms. Breathe in through your nostrils and visualize the breath flowing out through your hands. Be aware of any sensations in your arms and hands as you continue this exploration.

Focus on your torso. Slowly and deliberately explore your chest, your spine, your abdomen. Breathing in and out, exploring, noticing all sensations or lack of sensations within your torso. Be aware of all sensations in your pelvis, your buttocks, your genitals. Keep your focus on the sensations in your body. Be aware of the touch of the air against your skin. Be aware of the texture of your clothing and its feeling on your body. Be aware of the pressure of your body against the seat on which you are sitting.

Focus deepening, exploration continuing, move your awareness into your legs and feet. Very slowly and carefully explore your legs and feet. Become aware of all sensation or lack of sensation in your legs and feet.

Now, expand your attention to your entire body. Become fully aware of your entire body, warmth, cold, tingling, tickling, pain, numbness. Become aware of all sensations. If there is pain or tightness in any part of your body, you can ease it by imagining that, as you exhale, you are breathing through that body part and the tension is riding out on the breath. If there is headache or tension in the head, you can move that energy by focusing on your awareness. Breathe out through the palms of your hands and allow the excess energy in your head to move freely throughout your whole body.

Feel yourself to be fully in your body. Sense your energy flowing through your body. Feel yourself to be firmly seated, rooted. Breathe in. And out. Continue to pay close attention to your body. Now, notice if there is any difference in your body from when you began this exercise.

When you are ready, open your eyes.

Exploring Feelings

As you work with the breath and pay close attention to body sensations, you may notice deep feelings coming to the surface, sometimes with astounding intensity. "Exploring Feelings" is an exercise which gives us an opportunity to work with feelings in a new way. In this exercise we experiment with understanding feelings as energy that simply comes and goes. To be a witness to feeling, just watch, without trying to suppress or express emotion. Feelings are necessary. They are the water element within us. When they are flowing they connect us to life. Feelings bring a richness to all we do. It is a part of being human to share in the joys and sorrows of others. We need to find ways to work with feelings so that we are neither acting blindly out of intense emotion nor coldly out of repressed emotion. When feelings are repressed they color all our behavior and limit our range of choice.

In this exercise you are asked to become aware of your feelings in this moment, and to carefully observe them. Another approach is to choose a particular feeling that you want to explore. You may be feeling great sadness, for example, and, instead of doing whatever you usually do when feeling sad, you can use this exercise to sit and watch the feeling. At first, this may seem strange to you, but try it a few times. I can assure you from my personal experience that the results can be amazing. I have learned that I don't have to be afraid of my feelings, that I can be much less attached to them. And this detachment allows me to act in a stronger, clearer way. There's more energy for me to use when I'm not filled with sadness, anger or fear. Remember, this is something to practice. This is a new way of being with feelings. Be patient and kind to yourself.

Find a comfortable sitting position and take a few minutes to sit with the breath. Now, become aware of what you are feeling in this moment. How are you experiencing feeling in this moment? Is there a feeling of joy, of sadness, of anger, of sorrow, of pain, of calm? Become aware of all the feelings. Watch the feelings and notice where they are located in the body. Is there any tightness or tension connected with any particular feeling? Sit quietly and observe the feelings.

Letting the breath flow, be quietly aware of feelings as they arise within the body/mind. Notice whether the feeling moves from one place to another in your body. Does it feel stuck or is there motion? Does the feeling change? What does it become? How is the change experienced?

Now, take one particular feeling and make a close and careful observation of it. Is there a particular location in the body that is associated with the feeling? Is there a particular thought or image that is associated with it? Feel the feeling as fully as you can. Does it feel hot or cold? Is it hard or soft? Is the feeling contained or do you experience it throughout your whole body? Keep breathing with the feeling. Accept the feeling without trying to push it away or to keep it constant. Simply let the feeling be. Observe it as a process without identifying with it. Think "feeling" rather than "this is my feeling." Observe the feeling, feel the feeling without identification or attachment. Simply feeling. Feeling. Feeling.

Let the exploration go deeper as though the feeling were a huge onion and you are peeling away its layers. What is under layer after layer? What is happening? When the onion is peeled away, what is left ?

When the feeling has changed, released, or transformed, sit with the breath for a few minutes and notice whether there is any difference in your body/mind. If the feeling has not changed, released or transformed, simply know that it is feeling, a changing process of body/mind. While it has not changed in these moments, it will change sooner or later.

When you are ready, open your eyes. Be aware of any differences in feeling in the next few minutes, hours and days that may be connected to your having done this exercise.

Exploring Thoughts

We can work with thoughts in the same way we work with feelings or breath — making them an object of concentration. Thoughts, like feelings, come and go. When we sit and give them our full attention, we discover things about ourselves. For many of us there is a constant chatter going on in the back of our minds. Usually it takes the form of an argument we are having with ourselves. We make a constant commentary on our lives— "You should do this or you shouldn't do that." Or, "You should have done this, not that." Sometimes this goes unnoticed even though it is affecting our actions. When we are sitting and trying to focus our attention on our breath or on some other one thing, this chatter can become very loud. Like any other habit, when we pay close attention to it, it will stop. To create more space in our minds, and, therefore, in our lives, we can try looking at thoughts just the way we looked at feelings — as energy that comes and goes. We notice that we are thinking or planning or reminiscing, and we watch it all happen. We often expend enormous amounts of energy labeling thoughts as good and trying to hold on to them, or labeling them as bad and trying to repress them. It can be a great relief to treat them as just thoughts, moving energy.

Sit comfortably, so that your spine is erect. Feel your abdomen working gently, your abdominal muscles pulled slightly in and up. Feel this support and allow your shoulders to rest with a slight pull back and down. Breathe deeply and release any tension from your body.

As you sit with the breath and observe its coming and going, you may notice that, from time to time, thoughts seem to pop into your mind. Let these thoughts be like clouds, arising and dispersing. Become like the sky, open and vast. Thoughts are clouds. You are the sky.

Continue to focus on your breathing. When thoughts come into your mind, bring your attention back to your breath. Know that thought is simply thought. Observe the thoughts coming and going, without judgement. No need to repress negative thoughts or to try to hold on to positive ones. Thoughts are thoughts, moving, changing.

You may want to observe a particular thought and notice what other thoughts are connected to it. You may notice that one thought plays over and over again in your mind. Pay attention to which are the dominant thoughts. What are the patterns?

Then, bring your attention back to the breath. Breathing and thinking. Breathing and judging. Breathing and planning. Thoughts coming and going.

Thoughts are clouds. You are the sky.

Exploring Images

In this exercise, we observe images as they rise and fall, just as we observed the breath or feelings. Our mind is continually creating images. We are most aware of these images during the relaxed, half-asleep period we experience just before falling asleep. This is when we have most access to these images. However, we can learn to be receptive to images in an alert state of mind as well. While most people involved in creative work know how to access this place, we can all become more in touch with our creative energy, whether we use it for writing, painting, dancing or living in a deeper and more balanced way.

In the second part of this exercise, I suggest that you pick a specific image to work with. By exploring a particular image we can find what it has to teach us. We think in images. Before we take any action, however simple, we first have a mental picture of it. Most often, the image isn't conscious. When we can make it conscious, we are more easily able to see the motivation behind our actions. When we are able to see which images we want to actualize and which we want to dissolve, we are able to expand our options.

> Sit quietly with the breath, aware of its coming and going, aware of the process of breathing, aware of breathing, no attachment. Find a natural and relaxed breath. Sense that "breathing is happening," rather than "I am breathing."
>
> Now, hold the mind lightly, that is, neither falling into intense concentration nor becoming so lax as to let confusion arise. In this mind space, allow images to arise. Observe the coming and going of the images of the mind. Watch the continuous movement of the mind's pictures. See each of them clearly, without judgement, without

thinking whether the image is good, powerful, fearful or disgusting. Simply see the images.

Sit in a deeply relaxed way, attentive without grasping, so the mind's images arise spontaneously and effortlessly. Watch these images as they float by like clouds in a vast sky. If there are no images or, if the images are dim, simply watch without trying to make anything happen. Watch the space and look for the place where the images arise.

Now, pick one image and let the exploration deepen. Follow the image, uncovering layer after layer, delving deeper and deeper into the mind's imagery, becoming sensitive to the layers and to any feelings, thoughts or sensations that arise in response to the image. If you are so inclined, communicate with the image, perhaps asking it what it has to teach you. Be aware of any tendency of the mind to superimpose old ideas and beliefs on the image. Let the awareness of the image and its teaching arise spontaneously within the mind's eye.

Play with the image now. If it is without color, give it color. If it is colorful, let it become black and white. If the image moves, let it be still. If it is still, let it move. Play with the image as though your are seeing it for the first time.

If it is a scary image, create a soothing image. If there is a sad image, create an image of joy.

You can play with the images in many ways. If you see a powerful image, try creating several more that feel powerful. Try creating its opposite. Try changing the position of different parts of the image. You can take a single image and follow it to its limit, creating images like and unlike it, changing the feeling you connect with it, rearranging its component parts. Trace the image, asking, again and again, "What is the root of this image? Where does it come from?"

Now, focus on the breath again and notice any images arising spontaneously. Don't try to change them in any way.

Sit with the images and when they become still or, when you feel ready, open your eyes. Be attentive to any changes in thought and feeling that may be connected to this exercise.

Exploring Our Environment

In "Exploring Our Environment" we turn our attention from ourselves as separate to ourselves as part of an environment, and then back to ourselves as separate. The aim of this exercise is to develop an awareness of the self as always in relationship to the environment. Many people are hesitant to focus on their own self-development because they fear that doing so will necessitate removing themselves from the world. Nothing could be further from the truth. When we look inside we find that we do not, and cannot, exist alone. We exist in relationship to all of life. Just as the systems of our bodies function in relationship to the whole body, we, as living human beings, exist as part of, and in relationship to, the Earth and all her creatures. When we really experience this on a gut level, we understand that what happens to the Earth happens to us. Our breath is not separate from the whole breath of life. If the Earth is poisoned, we are poisoned. We cannot really care for ourselves without caring for the Earth, for all her people and all her creatures.

> Feel yourself seated comfortably. Know that the Earth is beneath you and the sky is above you. Know that there is breathing. Become aware of the breathing. Explore the process of breathing without attachment. Simply, there is breathing. Realize that breathing is happening in this moment. Inhale. Exhale. Inhale. Exhale. Inhale. Exhale. Breathing is happening.
> Breathing in oxygen and energy. Breathing out carbon dioxide. Realize that the air you exhale mingles with the air all around. As you breathe in and breathe out, another person is also breathing in and breathing out that same air. Breathing in and breathing out. Sensing the exchange of energy, the exchange of air. One breathing in and out;

another breathing in and out. Is there a difference?

Become aware of the air, aware of the environment. Sounds, sensations, energy around and within. Within and without. Within and without. Is there a difference?

Breathing in air, oxygen. Breathing out, releasing. Complete cycle, complete circle, moving in and out, in and out. Is there a difference? Become conscious of the sky above, the stars shining, visible at night, not visible in the day. Are they always shining? Sense the sun, high above. Feel the sun shining upon you. Be conscious of the sun shining upon another and another and another. Be conscious of the sun shining upon all life, all creatures, all beings. The sun is shining on the Earth.

Breathing in and breathing out. The process of breathing. Breathing is happening. Aware of the weather. If there is rain, hearing the rain. Knowing that each flower, each tree, each bush, receives the same rain, yet absorbs only its needed amount. Breathing in and breathing out.

Breathing in and breathing out. If there is wind blowing, hearing the wind. Wind — the unseen force. Wind, air. Wind blowing the clouds across the sky. Wind transforms. Wind transforms. Being aware of the wind.

Breathing in and breathing out. Aware of the whole environment. One breathing in, breathing out; another breathing in, breathing out. Same planet, same process, same sky. Breathing in and breathing out. Is there a difference?

Breathing in and breathing out. Attention to the environment. Calm, careful attention to the total environment. Breathing in and breathing out. Is one more deserving of the breath than another? Is one more deserving of the sun than another? Is one more deserving of the rain than another? Breathing in and breathing out. Sensing the whole environment. Aware of the whole environment.

Breathing with all of life, sensing the flow of life, sensing the continual exchange of energy. Becoming aware of the preciousness of life. Seeing what we receive from the Earth. Feeling connected and sustained by the Earth.

Recognizing the Earth as home. Who lives at home? Whose home is the Earth? Breathing in and breathing out. Sensing what we receive from the Earth. What can we give the Earth? Recognizing what we receive from the Earth. Where is the exchange? What is given? What is received? Breathing in and breathing out. Following the breath. Seeing, sensing, feeling the exchange of breath, exchange of air, exchange of energy. Breathing in and breathing out.

V
Loving, Forgiving, Releasing

You hear the sound of water and you know where
you want to be
Why wait? You've gone places you regret going
for money and such. Don't do that again,
Water says, Live here.
Don't carry me around in buckets and pans.
False duties. Rest and be quiet.

—Rumi[1]

Rumi, the ecstatic Sufi poet, speaks beautifully of living in the moment. We get so caught up in the rush of our daily lives, all the plans and activities, that we forget the only moment we really have is the present. Many people think they are living in the moment when they are actually running from one moment to the next. In fact, they are torn with desire and grasping at whatever seems to serve the momentary interest. Living in the moment requires a deep commitment. We must have the courage to forgive the past so we can focus body, mind and spirit on the task at hand.

How do we find the clarity that will enable us to live this way? My teacher, Dhyani Ywahoo, says that "forgiveness is the healing balm." The only way we can be fully present, the only way we can remember our true nature, is through forgiveness. She calls the process, "the stream of forgiveness, the stream of remembrance."

The element of water has long been associated with birth, rebirth and renewal. Ancient philosophers called water the first element, the mother of all things. "Most myths placed the primary impulse of creation in a watery womb of chaos or formlessness representing the Great Mother."[2] So we can think of returning to the water as a return to the Mother, the creator of all things. Washed with water, we are reborn. We are washed with the creative energy of the universe. We are washed clean of whatever prevented us from acknowledging ourselves as creators, the mothers of our lives.

Some Israeli friends shared with me a ritual they remember from childhood. It is the ritual of "Tashlikh," which means to throw. On Tashlikh, a holy day that follows Rosh Hashanah, the Jewish New Year, the people go together to a body of water and there they empty their pockets. They throw away every last bit of lint and dust in a gesture symbolizing discarding unfinished business and unresolved feelings. This community ritual is in preparation for making peace, for the most sacred day of atonement, Yom Kippur.

In the workshops my partner, Shuli Goodman, and I lead throughout the country we have created a similar ritual. If we are indoors we place a huge bowl of water on the floor and form a circle around it. Then we move around the water, slowly at first, calling out, in turn, what we wish to release. As the ritual deepens, voices blend together as we sing out, "I release pain. I release doubt. I release fear."

To the extent that we are able to release, to forgive and to love, we awaken. As we awaken, we are infused with an even greater sense of love, eventually with a love that needs no object. It simply is. We love, like the rose gives its perfume, because that is our nature. In loving, we experience a warm, abundant, connecting, expansive energy. Love has been called the "cosmic glue" — the force that holds the universe together.

Everything we say or do comes either from a sense of loving connection or from a place of fear, a withholding or twisting of that connection. Fear, in all of its manifestations — anger, greed, hatred, denial, aggression — limits us. Love, in all of its manifestations — joy, connection, peace, courage, integrity — frees us.

When we awaken to the loving energy of the universe, we come to understand that we are not separate entities. We can no longer allow any child to go hungry. It makes no difference whether that child is next door or in a country that is thousands of miles away from us. We can no longer say, "I'll feed my child, but not your child." We no longer think about the Earth, we think as the Earth.

> How can you not forgive yourself
> for being exactly as you are?
> To find the God within you
> you must go through the portal of self acceptance
> as you are now.
> Yes, all your faults and imperfections,
> all your little secret, fearful uglinesses
> that you are loath to admit to yourself
> are already known.
> They are part of the Divine Plan.
>
> True acceptance is saying, "It's all right,
> it's all right, it's all right."
> —Emmanuel[3]

Self Forgiveness

Loving and forgiving begins with ourselves. Until we forgive ourselves, we can't really forgive anyone else. The "Self-Forgiveness" exercise I've included here can be done as a visualization or it can be made into a ritual in which you actually do go to the edge of a pond on the night of a full moon. There are various levels in between pure visualization and actual ritual that lend themselves easily to this exercise. We might, for example, take a moment in our morning shower to recognize the healing power of water, to feel any blame or guilt we may have been holding being washed away as we forgive ourselves. .

> Watch your breath as it slows and deepens. Allow it to move by itself, without force. Just the act of witnessing the breath brings the awareness to a calm place. Breathe in and breathe out. Breathe in and breathe out.
>
> Know that you have waited for this time and that this is a very special ritual, a healing, a cleansing, in which you will partake. It is the ritual of forgiveness. A healing will happen on this night, when the moon is full. You are alone as you walk through the woods, without hurrying, yet not pausing; simply moving along, following the moonlit path until you come upon the still forest pool.
>
> You look up to the moon and back down to the Earth. Then your gaze moves again, this time from the Earth back up to the moon. You acknowledge Earth and moon as your silent witnesses. With a prayer of thankfulness, you bend down and touch the water. A splash echoes through the night, soft ripples move outward. You drink for those who went before you, and for those who will follow you. Then, you drink for yourself. A clear, fresh taste on your lips. You step out of your clothes and slow-

ly enter the pool. Each motion is deliberate, graceful. You are engaged in the act of forgiving yourself. Each time you dip into the water, you repeat your name, saying, "I forgive you. I forgive you. I forgive you." Again and again, you dip into the water, repeating your name, first silently, then aloud, washing away your guilt, washing away your tears, washing away the pain of the past, the fears of the future, allowing yourself to be all that you are. "I forgive you," you repeat again and again, washing the pain away. Dipping in the water, again and again, washing away, releasing, forgiving, letting go.

When you feel that the act is complete, you walk out of the water, toward the edge. You breathe deeply and drink in the moonlight, reflection of your beauty, reflection of your love.

Taking the small vial of oil you carried with you in your clothes, you begin to anoint yourself. You touch each place gently, saying your name and "I love you. I love you. I love you." You anoint your forehead, your throat, between your breasts. Gently anointing your body and repeating again and again, "I love you."

When the ritual is complete, you step into your clothes. You pause again, looking from pool to moon and moon to pool, giving thanks, standing in silence.

When you feel ready, you walk back down the forest path on which you came.

Loving Self, Loving Others, Loving Earth

The second meditation in this chapter is a version of the wonderful Buddhist Metta or Loving Kindness Meditation. There is a monk named Anando Thera who travels around the world teaching only the Metta meditation because he sees such a strong need for this practice at the present time.

> Begin with an easy awareness of the breath. Breathing in and breathing out. Breathing in and breathing out. Now, as you inhale, say to yourself, "May I be whole." And, as you exhale, say to yourself, "May all people be whole." Breathe in, "May I be whole." Breathe out, "May all people be whole." Continue to breathe in and out in this way as you say again and again, "May I be whole. May all people be whole."
>
> Now, as you continue breathing, begin to share your good wishes for the wholeness of all people with each member of your family. Let a quick mental picture of your parents appear, whether they are living or not, and wish that they be whole. Very gently moving through your family, wishing that each one be whole. See your partner, your brothers and sisters, your children and your grandparents. Breathe in and breathe out. Continue wishing each family member good health and well-being, wishing each of them wholeness. Visualize your aunts, uncles, cousins. See each of them and their families and wish them wholeness.
>
> Continue to breathe deeply, visualizing your dear friends, your spiritual community, your spiritual teachers. Wish each one wholeness. Send clear and loving thoughts

of well-being to each one.

Come again to the breath. Inhaling, "May I be whole?" Exhaling, "May all people be whole." Now, visualize someone that you need to forgive and say, "I forgive you." Forgiving them again and again with each exhalation.

Focus again on the breath. Breathing in, "May I be whole," and, breathing out, "May all people be whole." Picture someone of whom you need to ask forgiveness, and ask them to forgive you. Asking forgiveness again and again with each exhalation.

Come again to the breath and see an image of yourself. Repeating your own name, say, "I forgive you. I forgive you," forgiving yourself again and again with each exhalation. Exhale forgiveness from every cell of your being. "I forgive you. I forgive you."

Bringing your attention back to your breath again, inhale, "May I be whole." Exhale, "May all people be whole." Breathing in and breathing out, wish yourself and all people, wholeness.

Now, envision this beautiful planet. See it from above, as though you were looking down upon it from very far away. As you exhale, wish the Earth wholeness. "May the Earth be whole. May the Earth be whole." Exhaling. Wishing well-being and renewal for the entire planet.

Coming again to the breath, inhale. "May I be whole." Exhale. "May all people be whole." Inhale. Breathe in and receive wholeness, fill yourself with light and love. Exhale. Breathe out wholeness for the universe, your breath traveling farther and farther out, encircling the planet.

Healing the Inner Child

There is a little child who lives within our hearts. I see this child as one of the faces of the dancer. The child is the embodiment of love, creativity, curiosity and joy. The healthy child, the whole child, infuses our energy so that we meet life with a lighthearted playfulness. Each situation is new. There are no preconceptions. The child is a bold explorer. When she is free, we are unafraid to take risks. We delight in exploring our bodies, discovering and testing our strengths and limitations, and we bring our delightful sense of inquiry to the environment around us.

By the time we reach adulthood, many of us are harboring an inner child who is hurt and afraid. We cannot grow into our maturity, our wholeness, until the inner child is healed. Too often, she is screaming for love and attention. Her unmet needs translate into behavior that is limiting or destructive. Her natural love and gaiety are repressed. When we were very young, we were helpless and dependent and, for many of us, our childhood experiences were sometimes overwhelming. As adults we may react to situations in some way similar to our childhood situations as if they are life threatening. Had we been abandoned as babies, we would have died. If we are abandoned as adults, we can survive physically but, emotionally, we may feel as though we will die.

We are receptive beings. We have recorded in the memory cells of our bodies every message we have ever received. We continue to respond to these messages long after their original occasions have been forgotten. Some of the messages are helpful, vital to our health and well-being. These are living affirmations, the power and strength of which infuse all aspects of our lives. Other messages may have been twisted, mixed, limiting or destructive. Perhaps we had parents who, although they really loved us, were unable to see us as who we are. We could feel their love and, at the same time, feel unheard and unseen. Long after these childhood experiences are forgotten, we may find ourselves in relationships in which we experience a confusion about being loved and seen. We may carry certain expectations, manifested as a defensiveness, regarding whether a loved one really appreciates or knows the "real me." Some of our parents may have encouraged us to develop ourselves, to take advantage of opportunities they never had while, at the same time, unknowingly projecting their own pain and dissatisfaction about their life circumstances on to us. Such a mixed message might cause us to fear success. As adults, we may experience conflict over completing our education or doing some other thing that we unconsciously consider would surpass what our parent was able to do. We may, unconsciously, be trying to protect the parent from feeling pain around unrealized dreams and aspirations.

Many of us endured emotional, physical or sexual abuse as children and some of us have translated that abuse into a feeling that the world is not a safe place or that people cannot be trusted or that we are bad or unworthy of love. Sometimes the memory of abuse is hidden, yet its pain infuses our life to the point that we are unable to trust or to develop and sustain intimate relationships. Even when the abuse is remembered, sometimes it is not consciously connected with present life experiences as in the case of an adult who is unable to set goals or to make commitments but who has no idea of why she cannot do so. Sometimes those of us who were abused as children cope in other ways, becoming over-achievers or constantly trying to prove our inherent goodness.

Our inner child may have been silenced by such messages as "You're too old for that," or "It's time to take yourself seriously," or "There's no time for fun and games anymore." The pain created from denial of our joy and spontaneity can create limiting emotional patterns.

The pain of the little child must be healed so that natural love and creativity can bubble through us. We can learn to care for the hurt parts of ourselves as a loving mother would care for a frightened child. If the child part of ourselves is made to feel ashamed this will only increase the pain. Love, patience and sensitivity will ease the pain and humiliation and allow the loving and playful child within to re-emerge.

Our work with forgiving and releasing involves going back to childhood experiences in order to heal the hurt caused by what our parents, teachers and other adults in our lives did or did not do. To stay in a place of blame will not heal us. The act of blaming keeps power outside ourselves. We see ourself as victim, one who is powerless to change. Healing requires a transformation of our identity as victim. Healing comes with the recognition that the person we can change is ourselves and that we have the power to change.

As I explore my own power to change and heal, I find it helpful to see myself as a human being who is whole and who is in the process of uncovering that wholeness. This perception of myself allows me to forgive myself for mistakes I make, for things I leave undone. As I am able to release limitations and to forgive myself, I am able to forgive others, to see others as also in the process of uncovering their wholeness. Dhyani Ywahoo explains that Native Americans are very careful in their speech to recognize the wholeness that exists in everyone. Human beings are essentially whole, although their actions may be limited or destructive. Native Americans will say, "He acts like a mean man," rather than, "He is a mean man."

There are times when we may be unable to see the whole picture or to understand why a particular behavior is occurring. Our own pain or misunderstandings may be expressed through negative judgements, criticism or blame. The habit of blaming must be transformed for healing to occur. Not blaming, however, does not mean that we are incapable of recognizing what is appropriate and inappropriate behavior. When our energy is not twisted into blame, we are able to think, speak and act clearly. We know when behavior is unacceptable whether we are looking at a personal or a global situation. Forgiveness does not excuse or condone abusive behavior. Forgiveness releases us from limiting patterns so that we are open to expressing the power of love that is within us.

We can heal the inner child when we stop wishing for the parents we never had. If there is a longed for childhood experience we never had, we can have it now. The child energy in us is strengthened when we allow ourselves to be in the moment, to act spontaneously, to take risks, to be silly, to have a good time. Affirmations of our inherent goodness, playfulness and creativity will help in healing the inner child.

As adults, one of the ways we can re-parent ourselves, is through visualization. We can heal the inner child by visualizing this child and sending her love and appreciation. We can see the old experience, imagine erasing it, and then create a new experience that is loving and whole. In this way we can transform the pattern of blame, anger and hurt. It takes courage to look at what happened to us in the past and to choose to no longer respond to that pain. Through visualization, we create a new experience which becomes encoded in our memory cells. Then, we continue to let the transformative, affirming experience infuse our actions, rather than the harmful or limiting one. In working with visualization it is possible to deepen our understanding of such experiences so that we can see the many subtle ways we are responding to old messages. This is important work that has to be done again and again, as we let go of layer after layer of limitation. The focus of the following exercise is not to relive the original pain. It is to acknowledge it and transform it. The focus is not on how or why it happened. The focus is on our perception of what happened and how that perception continues to affect our lives. In transforming this perception, we re-parent ourselves. We come to see, to sense and feel ourselves as loving, worthwhile human beings. "Healing the Inner Child" is an exercise that will allow us to get in touch with the softness and the joy. We can reclaim our birthright of love.

> Visualize a beautiful color. Imagine that this color is the color of the air surrounding you. As you inhale, inhale this color. Breathe deeply and draw this clear, vivid, colorful light into your body. Feel the healing power of this light. Feel its healing vibration as it spreads throughout your body. Feel every cell and atom of your being infused with this healing color. As you exhale, release

any pain or tension you have noticed in your body. Continue to breathe deeply and fill your body with this healing light. Know that each time you exhale completely, you are becoming clear, free of pain and fear.

Know that you are a receptive human being. You received many messages in your early life and you may still be responding to them even though you may have forgotten their original form or context. Know that you have the power to transform any early message that limits you. You now have the opportunity to re-parent yourself. Right now, you will give yourself the love, the sensitivity and the understanding that is your birthright.

Now, imagine yourself seated in a most beautiful and comfortable space. In your arms you are holding a tiny infant. This infant is you, your child self. Look into her eyes and share with her the deep love and compassion you feel for her. Imagine the light and love which is shining in your eyes. Extend a warm and loving welcome to this tiny infant. Celebrate her. Enjoy her. Appreciate her. Love her. Welcome this sweet, wonderful child to the Earth. Acknowledge her gifts, her wisdom, her love. Affirm your willingness to be with her, to love, comfort and guide her, to enable her to actualize all within her potential. Hold the child. Love the child.

Now, let the image of the child fade into light and breathe all that light and love into your being. Allow the love you felt for that child and from her to fill your heart.

Continue to breathe deeply and to imagine yourself in a safe and beautiful place. Imagine yourself meeting a young child, a child who is between the ages of one and three.[4] This child is you. As you watch your child self, bring to mind a memory of some painful childhood experience. Let an image of this experience come before your mind. Now erase it. Breathe deeply and allow the energy of your healing color to again fill your heart and mind. Filled with a sense of healing, focus on how this childhood experience affects your present life. Bring to your consciousness both the obvious and the subtle effects of this experience. Remember all that you can. Then, let these thoughts and experiences leave your mind. Let them flow out on the breath of your exhalations.

Again, envision the young child and, this time, see yourself giving her what you would have liked to receive. See her and experience her receiving all the love and support and acceptance that she needs and wants. Be with that young child now and re-parent her. Give her the love and understanding that is her birthright.

Now, envision this young child as a child who is whole — happy and loved. See and sense and feel that child. Allow yourself to touch the energy of love, curiosity, exuberance. Allow yourself to feel the energy of this playful, loving child. Know that this carefree, energetic, spontaneous child is alive within you.

Affirm your connection with your inner child. Tell her that you will love her, care for her, and protect her. Whenever you are feeling scared, or lonely or sad, you can tune in to your inner child and give her the love and reassurance she so badly needs.

In this way the child within you will bring her joyful presence to every aspect of your life.

Releasing Judgement

This visualization, "Releasing Judgement," is one of my favorites because of the fantastic imagery called forth when people are asked to give shape to the voice of judgement within. Some have experienced this voice as fire or wind; others as tribunals or judges; others as stern, authoritarian figures; still others as wicked or fearsome monsters. However the judge appears in your mind, we can all be certain that we have one, that, at one time or another, we have suffered from the harsh criticism or judgement of others. And, to our dismay, we sometimes discover that the harshest judge of our own behavior, thoughts and feelings is ourself.

We use this visualization to release years of miseducation and misunderstanding. We have been taught that to grow we must continually have our shortcomings pointed out to us — and not necessarily in the most loving way. How many of us have endured ridicule and mockery during our years in the educational system?

In fact, to grow and change, we need to find clear ways of validating our own strengths and giving each other good direction. We need to teach by offering an example, by showing the way, and by allowing enough space for ourselves or others to try without fear of humiliation. If we want our children to be strong, loving adults, we must share with them what is acceptable behavior and what is not, without ever withdrawing our love and support from them. The language we use is important. We would do well to pay attention to how many times we say "don't" rather than "do." How many messages do we give a child about her inability rather than about her ability? How many were we given as children and how have they affected us?

The following exercise gets us to look at the ways in which we have been judged and the ways in which we have internalized judgement. It ends with a meditation for forgiveness, for we must always remember that forgiveness is the healing balm.

In your mind, follow the path your breath takes as it moves deeper and deeper into your body. Inhaling and exhaling. Inhaling and exhaling. Allow the breath to flow deeper and deeper into the body. Imagine the breath traveling throughout your entire body. Imagine it moving through each part of your body. It is feeling for an opening, looking for a sense of softening, of releasing. Continue to breathe through each body part.

As you breathe through your body, you may come to a place that feels tight or tense or painful. There may be a holding here, a blockage of energy. Go deeper into your breathing and come to the particular place where you hold judgements in your body. It may be in the tightness of your jaw, in the hunch of your shoulders, in the pit of your stomach. Find the place in your body where you hold all the judgements that have been passed on you by others.

Now, breathe into that tight place, feel the flow of your breath opening that space, and allow an image of a judgemental figure to appear in your mind. This figure may be someone you know and whose judgements you have experienced or it may be a mythological figure representing the judge. Let this judge appear before you and allow yourself to feel the pain of being judged. Hear the judge pronouncing the many judgements you have felt throughout your life.

Now, see those images slip away with your outgoing breath. With each exhalation, allow those images to be released from your body/mind.

Feel yourself going deeper into this experience. Become aware of the ways in which you have internalized the judge. See, hear and feel the judgement you have made on yourself. See, hear and feel the judgements you have made on other people. Is there a difference? Become aware of the internal judge and allow it to escape from your body/mind each time you exhale.

All the thoughts of "You should have known better," "You could have done more," "You shouldn't have done that," — allow all these thoughts and the feelings that accompany them to come into your consciousness. Bring to the surface all the ideas that you weren't good enough because of who you are, how you live, what you believe. Experience now all the ways that judgements have limited you, have harmed you, and begin to let these thoughts and feelings escape with each out breath.

Moving yet more deeply into the experience, allow the image of the judgemental figure to be erased. Allow the judgemental voices to be silenced. Let the pain of separation, the pain of judgement, be released more and more with each exhalation. Now, begin to forgive yourself for believing those judgements and for acting in a judgemental way, yourself. Repeat your name silently and say "I forgive you." Say and feel this forgiveness over and over again until you experience an actual release.

If there is someone else you need to forgive, see a mental picture of them and say their name over and over again, followed by "I forgive you." Say it again and again until you feel a release.

Now, focus again on your breath. Watch your breathing. Breathe through each part of your body and pay particular attention to the place where you had been holding the judgement before you let it escape. Direct a loving feeling to that place and to your whole body/mind. Breathe deeply and inhale the light of love, the light of forgiveness. Send warmth and compassion to yourself and to all people. Know that, if the judge returns, you can release it again. The process is complete, the process is continuous.

Breathe the light of love into your whole being.

Cleansing Rains

The visualization, "Cleansing Rains," works with the element of water as did the "Self Forgiveness" exercise. In this exercise, we have an opportunity for a non-specific release. We can just let go of our pain and shame without having to tie it to particular past experiences. All of us carry pain and shame, and, sometimes, it is a very heavy load. With this exercise, we can set down the load. We don't need to sift through it, to analyze it, or to understand it. We just know that we carry it and now we can let it go.

Breathe in an out, in and out. As you breathe in, hold the breath for a moment and, then, exale. Breathe in, hold and then release. Continue to breathe like this for several more cycles.

Now, imagine that you are outside, in your favorite place. Breathe in and enjoy the environment. Feel the richness of the Earth beneath your feet. Enjoy the sun and the breezes on your body. Breathe in and breathe out.

As you gaze up into the sky overhead, you notice that clouds are forming. As you watch, the sky becomes more and more cloudy and dark. You know that it will rain soon. You feel the tension in your body as the clouds sweep the sky. The wind becomes stronger, the sky darker. The pressure is building both within the air and within yourself. You are aware of the tensions and fears that are being held within you.

The sky darkens even more and a streak of lightning flashes across the sky. You hear the sound of thunder. More lightning and more thunder claps follow. At first they are in the distance, now becoming louder and louder as the rain approaches.

And the rains come — first a light sprinkling; soon a teeming rain. Within your body, you feel the release. Within your mind, you feel the release. As the clouds let forth the rain, all the pent up moisture is released. The Earth is grateful for the gift of rain. And you, as part of the Earth, receive that rain with joy. You feel within yourself a great release, a letting go, an outpouring of emotion. You experience the freedom, the joy, in this natural act of letting go.

Feel the rain washing down upon your body, your being. Be aware of the rain washing down upon the Earth. Feel the comfort that comes from releasing long-held emotions; feel the freedom.

Gradually, the rain slows and stops. The sun peeks out from behind the clouds and there, arched across the sky, is a beautiful rainbow. Breathe in the light of that rainbow. Feel the joy of its colors. Its light is washing through you, breathing in each color of the rainbow; feeling the healing energy of that light.

Breathe in and breathe out. Breathe in and breathe out. You are washed clean, emptied of emotion. You are standing, now, in the pure light of the rainbow. Feel her healing rays as you open, more and more, to receive them.

And give thanks.

Peaceful Resolution

The final visualization in this series on "Loving, Forgiving, Releasing" addresses the fact that it is in our thoughts that we set the precedent for our actions. Whatever is created is first a thought. To act peacefully, we must speak peacefully and to speak peacefully, we must think peacefully. The exercise, "Peaceful Resolution," gives us an opportunity to make peace even with those people who are not willing to talk with us on the physical plane. It gives us a way to resolve resentments and misunderstandings from the past even when the people involved are no longer present in our daily lives. In working with it, we learn to be open and to let go of the emotional charge around miscommunication.

This exercise also teaches us communication skills which will be useful with those people with whom we are in direct communication. We learn to listen receptively, to stay centered in ourselves so that we can really hear what someone is saying to us without trying to explain or blame, only listen. It teaches us how to reflect, rather than to expect. Communication opens when we can demonstrate our understanding rather than projecting our demands onto the other person. This exercise helps us to let go of the "If you loved me, you should," or "If I do this, you should do that," approach to relationships. My partner calls this the "Monty Hall, Let's Make a Deal Syndrome." When we connect with another from the place of unconditional love, our relationships become joyful and harmonious.

In this visualization, we see ourselves and the other within an infinity symbol made of light. (An infinity symbol looks like the number 8 tipped over on its side, a horizontal number 8.) We are connected, yet within our own space. When we see ourselves and the other clearly in these interconnected circles of light, we begin to talk. We begin communicating from the heart, sharing our feelings and concerns.

> Allow yourself to settle comfortably into the rhythm of your breathing. Feel yourself flowing with the motion of your breath. Consistent change — ebb and flow. Watch the breath move without attempting to change it in any way. Simply be with the breath. Who is breathing?
>
> Now, visualize yourself in a place on this Earth, a place that feels safe to you. Let it be a beautiful and calm space. Spend a few minutes feeling safe and at home in this space. Sense your connections with all of life. Feel the aliveness of the Earth. Feel your connection with the wind and the water. Know that you are a relative to every plant and tree. Know this connection extends to all of life, to every animal of the air, land and sea, to all the plants, to the rocks and minerals. Affirm your oneness with all of life.
>
> Now, visualize your friend here, in this space, with you. Sense her connection to all of life and to you. Visualize this connection as warm, pulsing light, spiraling around both of you in the shape of an infinity symbol. Visualize both of you within this infinity symbol of light. You are each within your own being, yet connected.
>
> Begin to speak from your heart to your friend. Affirm your connection, your unity. Affirm your desire to have clear, open and honest communication so that you can resolve any conflicts. Share with her your thoughts and feelings about your relationship. What are your concerns? What is happening now? What would you like to see happen?
>
> Sit quietly and wait for your friend to speak. Listen with an open heart as she responds to you. Be aware of your breathing as she is speaking. If she says something that is not comfortable for you to hear, notice what happens to the rhythm of your breathing and be aware of any sensations in your body. As you focus on what she is saying, stay attuned to how you are feeling.
>
> Continue to explore your relationship together, what

you enjoy, what is important to you, and what you would like to change. Explore how that change could happen. Ask yourself if you are willing to make those changes. Ask your friend if she is willing to make some changes.

When you feel the communication is complete for the moment, thank your friend for joining you in this experience. Ask her if she is willing to meet you again and decide with her how often and when you should meet. If you make no agreement for future meetings, thank your friend again for being with you at this time. Then, see your friend leaving the space.

Now, see yourself alone again in the space. Affirm again your connection in the full circle of life. Breathe deeply, focusing on your breath for a few minutes and, then, return to your usual consciousness.

VI
Transformation

The way to transform violence
back into the beautiful Light force
that it truly is
is the exquisite task of seeing violence
not as it presents itself, but as the force
that it will ultimately become.
There is a key here for all of you:
see even in the most despicable
the Divine quality that has become distorted.
—Emmanuel

The open heart, freed from fear, experiences the world in all its mystery and brilliance. All of us need to become alert to the wonders of the universe, to practice "awe-robics," like Lilly Tomlin's character, Trudy. Trudy, in her madness, is able to experience the invisible and wondrous connections in the universe. In *The Search for Signs of Intelligent Life in the Universe*, Trudy stops to look at the stars and says:

"I felt in awe. And then I felt even deeper in awe at this capacity we have to be in awe about something. Then I became even more awestruck at the thought that I was, in some small way, a part of that which I was in awe about. And this feeling went on and on and on.... My space chums call it 'awe infinitum'.... I decided I would set time aside each day to do awe-robics. Because at the moment you are most in awe of all there is about life that you don't understand, you are closer to understanding it all than at any other time."

I am in awe when I realize that the basis for life is love, complementary connection. We can find this connection even on a cellular level. When we look at the shape of the DNA molecule, the building block of life, we see a ladder twisted into a helical shape, like a spring. One side of the ladder goes up and the other side goes down. The rungs of the ladder are composed of complementary pairs of nitrogen bases. And, when each gene replicates, the mother gene doesn't die. It is subsumed intact by the daughter gene. Each of us houses within our bodies, then, some of the original genes formed millions of years ago when the universe began!

How do we practice awe-robics? How do we transform the fears that limit and separate us into the love, joy and courage of our being? We can begin this transformation by having a close look at our language. Our language is based on Aristotelian logic which stresses separation and linear cause and effect. It practically marches. We need to create a new language, one that dances, that expresses a reality of reciprocal and changing relations. We have so many words to describe a seashell or the sea. We need words to describe the relationship of the seashell to the sea. We can begin to choose our words with care. We can choose words that affirm life, abundance, and connection.

As we begin to speak in a positive way, we find ourselves more able to look for the positive, the gift, in every situation.

We can also become more aware of our perceptions and, like a gardener planting seeds, we can plant thoughts. We can carefully nourish these thoughts just as we nourish our gardens. Just as the soil is enriched by decaying vegetation, the fertile field of mind is enriched by the decaying of limiting habits and thoughts. We know that for seeds to grow they must have the proper balance of soil, nutrients, water, darkness and sunlight. Our new thoughts must be tended as carefully as seeds. The soil in which they take root can be fertilized with our old concepts and beliefs; we can spread them over the garden, like compost. And we must remember that newly planted seed-thoughts gestate in darkness and silence. If we run out to pull up a seed immediately after it has been planted because we want to see how it is growing, we will kill it. Likewise, thoughts must be given time to take root in our hearts and minds before we expose them to sunlight. When they are strong enough, when they are firmly rooted in our hearts, they will begin to inform all of our actions.

A powerful way of allowing seed-thoughts to take root is through affirmation. By stating something simply and positively over and over again, aloud or silently, we find that it begins to be the truth. At first we may feel separate from the affirmations. We may feel that they are untrue. Yet, if we are willing to suspend doubt and judgement in order to work with the affirmations, within a few weeks we will notice a change. The old, negative, voices will become quiet. The affirmations we repeat, the seed-thoughts, will join our everyday consciousness. Our perceptions of self and of others will change and we will respond in a more wholesome way to life.

When creating affirmations, state them simply, with strength and conviction. Use positive words in the present tense. For example, say, "I am," rather than "I think I am," or "I am going to be." Work with one or two affirmations at a time. Write them on a piece of paper and hang them where they can be seen easily — above your desk, on your mirror, on your refrigerator. Repeat them often, as you move through your day, while waiting for your car to warm up on a cold morning, while waiting in line at the supermarket, while walking down the street. The more you work with the affirmations, the more powerful will be the results.

You can make up your own affirmations to transform whatever attitudes you decide to change. As you work with affirmations, you will come to have a sense of how to create your own and to make them effective in many situations.

Some Suggested Affirmations

To transform fear — Courage is the natural state of my being. I am open to the abundant, loving nature of the universe. I am one with all that is. I inhale love, I exhale fear.

To transform feelings of scarcity — I am thankful for my life. I have all the time, energy and resources to do whatever needs to be done. Life is a full and rewarding experience.

To transform doubt — I am filled with a sense of inner security and safety. I know what needs to be done and I am able to do it. I am clear, compassionate, and skillful.

To transform anger — I inhale connection, I exhale separation. I act in harmony with all of life. I am honest, clear and loving when I communicate with others. I am love. We are love. I am peace.

To transform envy — I am whole within myself. I have all that I need. I rejoice in your good fortune. I am connected to and share all the goodness of the universe.

The Gardener

The act of affirmation is the act of consciously choosing which thoughts, which beliefs, we want to energize. A little poem I received from the Insight Meditation Center in Barre, Massachusetts, expresses this idea very clearly:

> The thought manifests as the word,
> The word manifests as the deed,
> The deed develops into habit,
> And the habit hardens into character.
> So watch the thought
> And its ways with care,
> And let it spring from love
> Born out of respect for all beings.

Sometimes the old thoughts are so deeply imbedded in our psyches that we need to uproot them. The exercise, "The Gardener," works with the release and transformation of old thoughts and the planting of new ones. This is another exercise which lends itself easily to ritual. If you have space in your garden, you may want to make a little love garden or peace garden. The seeds you plant in it can represent those thoughts of love and peace you wish to affirm and actualize in your life. City dwellers, too, can make an indoor garden, using flower pots to plant their seeds of clear intention.

Allow yourself to become transformed. Work with this exercise and with affirmations often. Think carefully about how you want your life to look. What are the values you want to nourish? What are the attitudes and qualities you wish to affirm?

Let your breath be slow and deep. Imagine that you are a great tree with roots extending deep into the center of the Earth. Let your breath move down into your roots and, at the same time, out through your highest branches. Breathe deeply into your root. Let the energy from the

Earth travel through your roots and up through your highest branches, out into the sky above you. Breathe deeply. Let the light of the sun touch your branches, travel down through your trunk, deep into your roots, and flow out into the Earth.

When you feel fully grounded, in touch with both the Earth and the sky, become aware that in your heart/mind there exists a garden. Its fruits spring from the energy of your thoughts. As your breath sinks deep within your body, let your mind travel deep within until you find yourself in this garden of the heart. Now is the time to weed the garden, to uproot from the garden any thoughts that are limiting, any emotional patterns that are negative, any actions that are incomplete. See yourself pulling up, weeding out, those thoughts of fear, separation, scarcity and pain. As you carefully weed the garden, take time to bring to mind the ways in which these thoughts were strangling the beautiful plants in the garden. Weed the garden, aware that these weeds, these limiting thoughts, are no longer necessary. Throw the weeds onto the compost pile so that they can be used as fertilizer to help the new seeds to grow.

When you have uprooted all the weeds, imagine yourself spreading the compost over the garden. When the soil is ready, begin to plant new seed-thoughts, affirmations of courage, abundance and joy. Plant new seed thoughts of well-being for yourself and for all the Earth. As each new thought is planted, let its energy resonate like a mantra through your entire being.

Safe in the garden of the mind, let the new seeds take root. Affirm that they will feed all of life. Safe in the garden of the mind, allow the seeds to take root that they may be harvested for the good of all life.

Transforming Fears

Transforming the Energy of Fear

This is the first of three exercises having to do with the transformation of fear. This one works with fear as an energy of restriction or limitation. We place no judgement on the fear, no judgement about whether we "should" or "shouldn't" be afraid. In this exercise we do not trace the origin of the fear or look to see if it is "rational" or "irrational." Nor do we look to see who or what is creating the fear. Instead, we simply recognize that, at one time or another, everyone experiences fear. Fear blocks the free flow of loving energy in the body/mind and causes us to shut down. If we can learn to sense the fear response, the tightening, we can work with the breath to soften those tight places and release the energy. We can release or transform fear without knowing its cause. We stay right in the present: "I have fear. I am transforming it." Once we have loosened the tightness, energy begins to flow and we affirm our love and courage.

Focus on your breath. Watch as you inhale and exhale, inhale and exhale. Notice whether your breathing changes, but do *not* make any conscious attempt to change it. Simply observe the flow. Inhale and exhale, inhale and exhale. Stay with the breath for several minutes, until you notice that your mind has stopped talking and your awareness is fully on the breath. If your mind begins to talk again, bring your attention back to the breath. Mind images, feelings, sensations in the body — let them be reminders to bring your attention back to your breath.

Now, notice where there is fear, tightness, tension in your body and let your breath go to that place. Bring the fullness of your breath into the center of your fear. Sense that tight knot of fear and let your breath gradually open it. Feel the fear as a knotted muscle, and your breath as a gentle masseuse, kneading that tight, sore spot. Keep your breath flowing. Breathe in a glorious light from the universe, and exhale that light through the place of fear. Allow that place to gently open. Let the warmth of the light soften that place. Let the breath move gently through the fear. Feel that tight place loosen and open. There is no force, just a calm assurance that the breath is flowing through that area, however constricted, however tight. Gradually, the breath will open that space. Breathing, making more room, more space, letting the fear dissolve. Breathe in. Inhaling, letting the the warmth of the breath, like the sunlight, melt the fear. And you experience your fear melting to be like energy flowing, like a stream flowing through the body. What was once frozen solid, trapped, is now melting and begins to flow.

Keep the breath flowing. Notice if you begin to hold your breath and gently remind yourself to keep breathing. Keep breathing. The breath, like the warmth of the sunlight is melting the fear, and energy is again flowing. Keep breathing through the tight area until you sense an opening, a release of energy. The energy feels like a river, thawed, returning to the ocean. Flowing, flowing, returning to its source. When you feel space where there was once fear and tightness, bring your attention to each part of your body, in turn, being certain that energy is flowing easily through all of them. Sense the in breath to be like the rays of the sun, streaming down upon your head and let the energy flow downward through your whole body. Streaming light, rivers of light, dancing through your body. Rivers of light returning to their source. Light traveling, dancing, singing through your body.

As the light dances, as the rivers flow, sense that you are light. Feel yourself dancing, joining in the universal dance of life. The whole universe, alive, pulsating, vibrating light. You are open to and receiving this light. You are joined with this light. You are this light. You are the dance. Feel the affirmation sing through you as you dance: "I am light. I am courage. I am love."

Transforming Specific Fears
Fear of Driving

In this exercise, we work with a specific fear. Sometimes, as in the previous exercise, we work with the energy of fear, without specific content. Other times, it is appropriate to choose a specific fear and transform it by, in this case, imagining the feared situation as enjoyable.

Many people feel unsure about driving. They may be afraid of having an accident due to drunk or unskilled drivers or they may have already been in an accident. People may be uncomfortable driving at night because of lower visibility or a fear of having a breakdown in a deserted place. For some people a fear of being independent may manifest as a fear of driving.

In this exercise we do not explore the reasons for the fear. We focus, instead, on visualizing the feared situation as a pleasing situation. I have always been a rather reluctant driver myself, and have found visualization and affirmation extremely helpful. Visualizations, of course, cannot take the place of safe, skilled driving or having a safe, reliable car. They don't negate the need for reading road maps and having clear directions. What a visualization does do is to help us release blocked energy that prevents us from taking good care to do what we need to do in every situation.

We should start by doing this exercise in a safe space, away from the car. Eventually we may want to do it each time we get in the car to drive.

You can use the form of this visualization to create your own visualizations to help transform other specific fears that are of concern to you.

> Take several deep breaths. As you inhale, imagine that you are inhaling from deep in the center of the Earth. With each inhalation you are drawing the Earth energy up into your body. Earth energy is flowing through you. Imagine the base of your spine extending down into the center of the Earth, like a giant root. Through this root you receive the energy of the Earth.
>
> If there is any part of your body that feels tense or shaky, imagine a grounding cord, a root, extending from that place through the center of your body and into the center of the Earth.
>
> Now, imagine that you are walking toward your car. It is a very safe and reliable car, a car that is a pleasure to drive. Climb into the car, settle yourself comfortably, and fasten your seat belt. Put the key in the ignition and

turn the car on. As you wait for the engine to warm up, imagine a circle of warm love and protection surrounding yourself and the car. Breathe deeply and see yourself driving the car. See yourself enjoying the drive. Feel yourself relaxed and confident, a skilled driver. Spend a few minutes with this visualization. You are driving and enjoying the drive.

Breathe deeply and affirm, "I am a relaxed, safe and skilled driver. The road, the car, and I are one." Breathe deeply and repeat the affirmation several times.

Now, picture yourself reaching your destination, relaxed and confident. You get out of the car and stand on the Earth. Affirm, again, your deep connection to the Earth energy.

Return to your normal consciousness, relaxed and energized.

Changing Jobs

In this next exercise, we again work with a specific fear, in this case a fear some of us may have of leaving a job. This exercise gives us the opportunity to focus so that we can feel our fear or anxiety and, then, to relax enough to experience our deepest feelings about our present job.

Many people spend years in unsatisfying jobs because they are afraid of any change or, perhaps, they doubt their ability to do another job. Some feel they don't have the right to pursue a career of their choice. Some may be performing a certain job to please their parents or their partners or because they think that, as women, they can't do another job although they might prefer it. Some are tied to having to earn a certain level of income and fear that doing what they'd most like to do won't provide the financial support they need. In this exercise, we explore our own fears without judging them. We sit in a meditative state to contemplate questions concerning our jobs without trying to analyze any information that comes to us.

The next part of the exercise is a playful one. Here, we imagine the kind of job we really want without any of the if's, and's or but's. This kind of play frees us to find new ways of organizing our present skills or of obtaining new skills to enable us to get the job, or to create a job, that is in harmony with our life purpose. Change begins in the imagination. Once we have imagined something, we can work to make the possibility into a reality.

We complete this exercise with affirmations of our confidence, our skills and our right to have the job our heart desires.

Breathe in and breathe out, watching the breath as it comes and goes. Know that life is change, a coming and going. Breathing in and breathing out, allowing the breath to flow. Inhale and be born to each moment. Exhale, release, and die to each moment. One moment flowing into the next. Inhale, receiving new inspiration, new information. Exhale, letting go of the old, making way for the new. Inhaling and exhaling.

Notice where in your body you are holding tension. Sense any anxiety or fear as you continue to breathe deeply. Direct the flow of your breath to that tight place as you exhale. Feel the releasing. Feel the opening. As the breath flows through you, your fear, held in that tight place, is dissolving.

Now, picture yourself at work, doing your present job. Feel your feelings. What does it feel like to be at work? What are you thinking? Breathe deeply and let your thoughts and feelings about work come to the surface of your consciousness. Let your breath flow through your feelings. Feel how this creates space.

Stay with your feelings and thoughts. Explore them more deeply. Allow insight to arise as you reflect upon your present occupation. What will happen if I leave this job? What will happen if I remain at this job? What will happen if I get a similar job for a different company? What will happen if I do a different job for the same company? Going deeper, explore these questions and let other questions arise.

Now, let those thoughts and questions disappear. Allow yourself to feel clear. Breathe deeply and exhale completely. Create in your mind's eye the job that would be ideal for you. What would you like to do? How could you make the best use of your skills?

Picture yourself working in a way that would best serve yourself, your family, your community. Play with your visions.

Now, let these visions dissolve and return your focus to your breathing. Take a few deep breaths. Inhaling and exhaling. Let arise from within you an affirmation that will help to manifest a new job. Affirm that you have the right, the confidence, the skills, the energy to find or create and sustain a job that will be of benefit to yourself and to those around you.

Repeat the affirmation a number of times and then open your eyes.

Transforming Anger,
Another Face of Fear

Fire is an image I have found to be most empowering in thinking about anger. Fire is an activating force, a force that changes one thing into another. It transforms the clay into the pot and the grain into the bread. Through fire, the heat and pressure within the Earth, beautiful crystals are formed. We, like the crystals, need fire to bring us warmth and light, to polish us and refine our wisdom. The chance to learn to feed the fire, to work with the energy of transformation, is one of the gifts of being human. It is the energy of fire that enables us to extract from each moment what is essential for growth and to change the form of the remainder.

For many of us, it is only through anger that we are able to tap the power of our inner fire. The power of our anger may have become the driving force behind important changes in our lives. It may have been the power of anger that allowed us to separate from our parents, to begin to see ourselves as individuals with our own thoughts, feelings and beliefs. It may have been anger that enabled us to leave uncomfortable, and sometimes unbearable, situations. It was often anger that sparked the formation of important bonds — anger brought us together as women, as people of color, as feminists, as peace activists, as lesbians and gays, as civil rights workers, as revolutionaries.

We need the fire; we need its energy to move and to change. We need to recognize that anger is part of a process and to remember that, as a process, it must keep moving. If we continue to use anger to feed our fire, eventually we will burn out. Yet, if anger is the only way we know fire, when we suppress our anger, we suppress our fire. We then become depressed and unable to move or change.

A good way to begin working with anger is to view it as a form of energy. We may still be acting from the messages we were given early on that say, "Anger is bad," "Anger isn't nice," or "Anger will destroy us." Or, we may have turned those messages around, now believing that "Anger is good." Or, "We need anger in order to change." We can get stuck in either of those places. When we understand anger as energy, however, we see that it can be changed, transformed into something else.

When I work with the fire image, I see the wood that keeps the fire burning and I see the Earth out of which the trees grow. I am aware that to make any changes I need fire. I need energy, heat and light. I need to burn, to purify, to transform old habits and thoughts. When the fire burns wood, ashes remain. These ashes go back into the Earth, enriching the soil. Nothing is wasted. So the Earth is fed by our old attitudes, transformed into new soil from which new attitudes can grow. If the wood that feeds our fire is anger, then we must continually pull toward us hurts, injustices, whatever feeds the anger within us. Or we can go deeper still, back to the Earth and feel the Earth's energy nourish and support us. With this energy, rather than the energy of anger, we can make change. Now, the anger can serve as a warning that something is out of balance. When we heed the warning, we look to the Earth for the energy to act. We recognize the anger and are thankful for the warning. Then, we let our anger flow back into the Earth. As we breathe in the Earth's energy and exhale our anger, letting it flow back into the Earth, we are able to act.

In our daily lives we need to understand and appreciate anger. We need the courage to explore it. Only when we get to know it can we truly determine the form that its expression will take in our lives. This exploration is an ongoing process. Sometimes we find that the anger we are experiencing in the present is due to some unresolved material from the past. Other times, we may find that it is necessary to speak, to say what is acceptable for us and what is not. Another time, the exploration of our anger enables us to act. We have concern for the rights of children or elders. We want to provide safety from battering. We walk across the country for peace. We support educational projects. We organize at work. We grow community gardens. Release of anger is not release from responsibilty. Release of anger gives us the freedom to choose from a wide range of responses to a situation.

In this exercise, we look at a situation in our lives in which we experienced anger. We work with the specific sensation of anger in our body, releasing the energy of anger and renewing our connection with the Earth. From a new place of clarity and connection, we again envision a situation that could stimulate angry feelings. This time, we make a change in the situation. Again, we complete the exercise with an affirmation.

> Breathe deeply and allow yourself to relax as the full, deep breath flows through each part of your body. Inhale, drawing energy up through the soles of your feet and allowing it to wash through each part of your body. Energy of Earth flowing through each part of your body. You are relaxed.
>
> Now, remember a time when you were angry. See the situation vividly in your imagination. Recall the experience of anger. How did you express it? Did you scream, cry? Was your voice controlled and tight-sounding? Did you act as though you weren't angry, trying to push the feeling deep inside?
>
> Feel the anger in your body now. Is there a tightening of your jaw or fist? How does your stomach feel? How does your head feel? Is there a burning sensation anywhere in your body? Feel anger in your body at this very moment.
>
> Now, let the pictures vanish. The situation is no longer vivid. You have only the feelings in your body. Focus your awareness on the sensations in your body as you experience anger. Wherever there is a tightening, breathe through that place. Each time you inhale, draw the energy of the Earth up through your body. Each time you exhale, send the feelings of anger back down into the Earth. Continue to explore the sensations of anger as you breathe Earth energy through your body. The energy from the Earth will begin to dissipate the sensation of anger. Feel yourself grounded and supported by Earth energy. As you exhale, exhale the anger. As you inhale, bring new energy, new nourishment, into your body from the Earth.
>
> Continue to feel yourself rooted to and sustained by the Earth and, again, bring to mind the situation in which you felt anger. How would this situation change if you kept your awareness on the energy of the Earth and released the anger into the Earth? How would you act? What would you say and do? Allow yourself to feel sup-

port from the Earth

Keep the situation vividly before your mind's eye. Feel yourself in the situation and feel the support from the Earth. Do what you need to do. See and feel the anger being transformed into right action, action that brings harmony. Anger transformed into right action, action that is complete, action that brings balance. Inhale, and bring in the loving energy of the Earth. Breathe out clear action.

Now, slowly, dissolve all of the images and affirm: "I am connected to the Earth. My actions are clear and purposeful. I am connected to the Earth."

Transforming Envy/
Affirming Connection

Envy, like anger, can be traced to our feelings of separation and fear. We have become separate from our own creative source. We believe that the object of our envy has something that we don't have. The "other" is better, or stronger or more talented than we are. Unable to value ourselves, we project value onto someone else. They become worthy and we remain worthless. The other has the talent, the skill, the beauty, the wisdom, the finances we want. We may not all experience envy intensely, but the feelings of scarcity and fear which generate envy have been experienced, in some measure, by all of us.

Each of us manifests envy in different ways. It may drive us to compete, to try to develop or obtain for ourselves what the other has. In this case, the action we take might bring us what we desire, but the stress it creates can be unhealthy and may even lead to an increase in fear. Or, we may not compete at all. We may just feel discouraged, too helpless or hopeless to even try. We may be motivated by a feeling of scarcity, seeing resources, love, or success as limited, believing there is only so much and, once it gets used up, there is nothing left. When feelings of scarcity, fear and separation turn into envy, the envy may be expressed as greed and aggression. We struggle to obtain for ourselves what is limited and, then, we must protect what we have. This is a vicious cycle which is self-perpetuating.

The only way out is to affirm our own creative being and our connection with all of life. The potential, the power, the energy of life, exists within each of us, and each of us is connected to the others and to all of life. There is an exchange. This means that we can share in the good fortune of others. Each person's strength and talent are shared by us all.

In working with envy, as in working with all feelings, we acknowledge the feeling as an energy in our lives. We can explore the feeling and try to see its origin. If we find its origin in self-doubt, we can work with affirmations of our wisdom and certainty. If there is pain because of loss, or, if there is a feeling of hopelesssness, we work with these feelings. We also work with affirmations of our own strength and creativity. We acknowledge our connections to the Earth and to all of life. When we are able to let go of feeling separate (from our own creativity or another's), we find new reservoirs of energy available to us. With this energy we can begin to actualize our own creative potential.

Deepen your breathing. Inhale slowly, filling yourself with the energy of the Earth. Exhale completely, contracting your abdomen slightly so that you empty it totally of breath.

Visualize yourself in a very safe place, a place where you can do some important inner work. Relax in the beauty of your space. Now, picture a person for whom you feel envy. This person may demonstrate qualities you wish you had. This person may be living in a way that you wish to live. Without judgement or shame, allow yourself to feel the envy. Do you feel hurt? Angry? Separate? Whatever you are feeling, it is all right to feel it.

Now, erase the picture of that person from your mind's eye and dissolve your feelings of envy. Bring your awareness back to your breathing and affirm your inherent wisdom and creativity.

Repeat your affirmation a number of times and then, slowly, refocus on your breathing. As you breathe deeply, see a shimmering pyramid of light deep within the center of the Earth. As you inhale, light from this gleaming pyramid spirals up through your feet and legs, into the center of your body. With each inhalation, the light rises higher and higher along your spine. The light infuses your whole being. As you exhale, it streams from your eyes, your hands, your heart, and your feet. As you inhale, you receive this light and, as you exhale, you send this light out. Become aware of all life around you. Every plant and tree is also receiving this light from the Earth and radiating it back into the Earth. At the same time as you are receiving energy from, and radiating energy to, the Earth, you are also receiving and radiating energy from the sun. The sun's energy is also streaming through you and streaming from your eyes, your heart, your hands, and your feet. The same is true of all the plants and trees around you.

Now, see again the person you were envious of. See this person receiving energy from the Earth and sun and radiating energy from eyes, hands, heart, head and feet. Both of you are receiving and sending energy. There is a connection. There is an exchange.

You are enhanced by the good qualities and achievements of the other. The other is enhanced by your good qualities and achievements. You share in this light together.

As you continue to be nourished by this exchange of light, know that all people share in this exchange. See your family, friends, neighbors — all exchanging this light. Allow your vision to deepen and widen to include all people, all of life — sharing in this dance of light, this dance of life. Breathe in and breathe out, breathing the light, sharing in the light. Know that all deeds of integrity, strength, cooperation and love are shared by all. Feel strength in the knowledge of this connection. Feel affirmed by this connection. Feel the abundance of light and love within the universe.

Awaken with the knowledge of this light.

Transforming Attitudes and Beliefs

We can use the format of the final exercise in this section to explore and transform any belief or attitude. The example I use here gives us a chance to explore our attitudes and beliefs about money. Money, in this culture, is a source of much interest and some pain to many people. Either we feel we don't have enough or that we have too much. Depending on our belief system, we may feel that a person who has a lot of money is more deserving than another. Or we may feel that a person with money must have done something illegal or immoral to get it. Greed and aggression, the results of fear and withholding, have created an inequitable distribution of money and other resources. Often, the choices we make about how we spend money show little concern for the welfare of the majority of people or for the Earth. Our beliefs and feelings about money are intertwined with our feelings about scarcity, survival, power, sex, love and acceptance. I believe we cannot come into a clear relationship to money until we explore our feelings and attitudes about it. In the first part of this exercise, we look at what we believe about money and why we believe it. In the second part of the exercise we look at money as energy, energy which is the essence of everything in this universe. As energy, money must flow; there must be an exchange. We need money/energy to come to us and we need to have money/energy flow from us. How would we use money if it were thought of as energy to be shared, rather than something to be acquired as a badge of power and prestige? What does abundance mean? What does abundance mean specifically in relation to money? How much do we really need? How would money as energy look in our daily lives?

The affirmation in the third part of the exercise was given

to me a number of years ago and I have found it to be very effective. Sometimes we react to what we see as wasteful or oppressive attitudes about money by wanting to run away from having anything to do with it. We don't want to be abusive, so we don't want to have any money. If we have no money, then we don't have to deal with it. We may find that our fear of money is confused with our feelings of scarcity, unworthiness or fear. The so-called "Protestant Ethic" that infuses this culture is very connected to patterns of withholding and denial. Dhyani Ywahoo has said that, in the Native American culture, a person's wealth was considered to be a good thing — it meant they had more to share.

In a connected universe, what we do affects everyone and what everyone else does affects us. A recognition of this connection calls for the whole. The drawing toward us of money is a responsibility. True abundance comes from honoring reciprocity. We receive and, because we receive, we give. So it is in this spirit that the affirmation is given. The affirmation dissolves attitudes of withholding; it affirms financial reward as a blessing, as an opportunity to grow; and it acknowledges our ability to receive joyfully.

Each part of the exercise can be done alone or the entire exercise can be done at one time, as I've shown it here.

> Allow yourself to feel deeply rooted in the Earth. Sense the Earth beneath you as you inhale energy from the Earth. As you exhale, send that Earth energy into the sky. Inhale, and draw the sky energy into your body. Exhale the sky energy back into the Earth. Sense the cycle of Earth energy and sky energy meeting in your body, meeting in your heart. Let the practicality of the Earth meet with the visionary energy of the sky. Sense Earth and sky meeting in your heart.
>
> Travel deep within yourself to a place that is safe and comfortable. Travel to a place of solitude, a place where Earth, water and sky meet. In this place, you will explore some deeply held beliefs relating to money. Let your breath flow fully and easily — no stopping, no fear, no

holding. Just the breath, flowing easily and freely.

Sit quietly in this space and allow feelings and beliefs to arise as you complete these thoughts in your mind. Let your thoughts flow easily. Make no attempt to control them or to come up with "the right answer."

Money is . . . . Let your mind fill in this space.
Money is . . . .
I think having money means . . . .
Having very little money is an indication of . . . . .
Let your breath flow as you move even more deeply into this exploration of your beliefs relating to money.
When I was a child, my mother felt this way about money . . . .
When I was a child, my father felt this way about money
. . . .
Now that I am an adult, this is how my feelings about money are similar to those of my parents. . . . .
Now that I am adult, this is how my feelings about money are different from those of my parents. . . . . . .

Now, focus on your breathing and allow your thoughts to become calm and quiet. Take a few deep breaths. In this relaxed space, contemplate money as an energy within the universe. As energy, money is exchange. It comes and it goes. Money as energy is abundant and increases through being given and received. Breathe in and breathe out. Think of money as the breath — flowing, coming and going. You are always receiving money and you are always giving money. When you give money away, you receive money. When you receive money, you give money. Money is energy, there is always enough.

Relax with this knowing. Consider how this knowing will manifest in your life.

Now, bring your focus back to your breath. Take a few more deep breaths. Affirm to yourself: "I dissolve in my mind and in the minds of all others any ideas that my Goddess-given good can be withheld from me. Those financial blessings that are mine by Divine Right now come to me in abundance and I joyfully accept them."

Gradually let the affirmation fade away and bring your attention back to your breath. Sit quietly for a few minutes and then, slowly, open your eyes.

VII
Integration

We are the mirror as well as the face in it.
We are tasting the taste this minute
of eternity. We are pain
and what cures pain, both. We are
the sweet, cold water and the jar that pours.
—Rumi

We are complex human beings, each of us embodying our own variety of attitudes, habits, traits, abilities and beliefs. Sometimes we find that we hold beliefs or attitudes that seem to conflict with each other. While we may understand intellectually that we can be both compassionate and action-oriented in the world, emotionally we may experience these qualities as incompatible. We may feel that to be loving and caring prevents us from actively achieving some goal we have set for ourselves. Or, we may become so goal-oriented that we lose sight of feelings or relationships. Unable to see the connecting process, we become attached to the material creation, rather than living in the space where the spring of creativity is always flowing. Whenever I hear an old tape playing in my head, saying "Nice girls don't do that," or "It isn't spiritual to want this," I know I have some work to do. I need more balance and integration so that I can truly become all that I have the potential to be.

Our many diverse qualities bring richness and depth to our lives. We all have the ability to be powerful and compassionate, peaceful and wrathful, decisive and considerate, sexual and spiritual, thoughtful and spontaneous, ecstatic and intelligent, serious and humorous. Whenever we find ourselves caught in a struggle of either this or that, we can be sure the answer is neither. The answer, most likely, is another quality or possibility that combines both this and that and is more expansive than either. Moving from an either/or position to a both/and position is a process that is necessary if we are to become fully actualized human beings. It is challenging work, especially when so many of our culture's messages seem contradictory or polarized. We feel we have to choose one attitude or action over the other. We have forgotten that all polarities are an aspect of a single whole. To develop any one quality without balancing it with its opposite can be harmful.

One of my clients, a young man in his twenties, was dismayed by the fact that people always thought of him as a "nice guy." When I asked him to describe what a nice guy was, he answered, "Someone who is compassionate, non-judgemental, thoughtful, kind and polite." He described the bad guy as someone who put himself first, and was able to get what he wanted. This young man had strong values, yet there was a dullness or superficiality about him. His relationships seemed to lack passion. What had happened? In splitting qualities into good and bad, he was sitting on a lot of strength, creativity and virility. Afraid to take risks, he wasn't able to go deep into his work or to pursue the kind of relationship he wanted. My client needed to break loose, to take risks, to become wild, without being cruel.

The integration of a multitude of qualities is a challenge most of us face. One of the primary ways we tend to polarize our energy is in relationship to those qualities we see as male and female. With few exceptions, cultures, both Eastern and Western, consider the female nature as having to do with the feeling realm, the willingness to soften and open, to be receptive. The female is associated with the moon, the ability to reflect, to draw out, to magnetize. There is a sense of wonder and mystery surrounding the female nature. The male is associated with the realm of activity, bodily movements and expression in the outer world. Male energy is seen as active and analytical, embodying the ability to distinguish particulars, difference. Male energy is associated with the sun and the ability to radiate.

Female/moon and male/sun is the traditional view. There are some notable exceptions. In some Native American traditions, the sun is called, "She Who Shines." In the Jewish mystical tradition, the Kabbala, the qualities of receptivity and moon energy are related to the male. The active energy of the sun is seen as female. In Hindu iconography, the female creative force, Shakti, is the active principle. She is pictured dancing upon the horizontal Shiva, the receptive male principle.

What we are speaking of is life force energy, the currents of which manifest as receptive and active. The Chinese refer to the two kinds of energy as yin and yang. Native Americans speak of mother and father. Jungian psychologists use the terms anima and animus. It matters less what they are called than that we know that these currents of energy flow through every individual.

In exploring female and male energies the lines of demarcation are not as clear as they might first appear to be. The rigid separation of these qualities has indeed set the precedent for gender stereotyping. Rigid definitions of what is female and what is male have limited the actualization of the full range of human qualities within all of us. Eastern thought, even though sensing these qualities as complementary parts of a whole, has sustained more rigid stereotypes than has Western thought. With the advent of modern technology and especially the development of birth control, Western women have been freed from the drain of continuous child bearing, and, as women have gained access to education many of the myths about female and male stereotypes have begun to disappear. In this era we are more likely to conceptualize the healthy woman or man as androgynous.

Intuition, long considered the province of women, provides us with access to the energy of the universe. In denying intuition, we are denying the source of life. When we refuse to listen to intuition, the voice of the divine within, we greatly limit our creative expression in the world. The imbalance created by this denial has brought the energy of fear and destruction to the critical stage we are experiencing today. Unless all of us, female and male, begin to integrate the caring and nurturing aspects of life with purposeful action, the Earth cannot survive.

In Jewish mystical tradition, there is a teaching called "The Shattering of the Vessels," which says that during creation, the divine light burst through vessels that were meant to contain it. Fragments of the divine light were scattered throughout the universe. These fragments were known as "Shekhina," the feminine presence of God.[1] Now "Shekhina" is in "galut," in exile from home, from the wholeness of divinity. It is the task of humanity to come home, to reunite the divided mind, to bring together the female and male qualities.

I have found the metaphor of lover and warrior to be a helpful way to think about compassion and action. Compassion, without action, can cause us to stagnate; we can drown in feelings. Action without compassion can turn into aggression and cruelty. Feeling is necessary. It is the water element, the fluid connecting us, flowing into all of life. Where there is depth of feeling, there is richness in all we do. It is part of being human to be able to share in the joy and sorrow of others. The lover embodies the feelings that enable us to experience our kinship with all of life. This feeling of kinship is reflected in our ability to act in accordance with universal law. We consider the effect our actions have now and for many generations to come. The lover knows there is no act without consequence. The lover is our creativity, our ability to connect with, and express, the divine harmony in all we do. When the lover is awake our communication is clear and deep, from the heart. There are no barriers, no judgements, no expectations. The lover, attuned to all of life, feels the mystery of creation, listens to the voice in the water and on the wind. The lover is our joy, our compassion, our loving-kindness.

When the lover is undeveloped within us, we may feel disconnected from our deepest self and disconnected from others. We may relate to our lovers and friends through a bargain and exchange paradigm: "If you loved me, you would . . . ." We may be unable to form intimate relationships or we may seek to merge in our relationship in a way that causes us to lose a sense of personal integrity and authenticity. Or, we may act in collusion, supporting the unhealthy habits of each other.

The other aspect of the polarity is the warrior. The warrior is the embodiment of action. In the Castaneda books, Don Juan speaks of living our lives as warriors. This means that we see each situation as a challenge and respond fully without complaint or regret. It was from my reading of Castaneda's Don Juan books that I became conscious of the concept of impeccability — living with precision and total attention. So many of us live our lives concerned about what others think. The warrior is concerned only that each action be impeccable. When we bring the mind of the warrior to our lives, we act with clarity and purpose. Each act, however large or small, deserves our complete attention. What an enormous impact acting with this attitude would have on the rigid definitions of sex, race and class we have created.

The warrior is at war with all limitations, with every obstacle that prevents the realization of the authentic self. This battle to overcome limitations is a long and strenuous one. It is the central theme of all great scriptures, this battle between good and evil. The evil is the limitation, the doubt, the restlessness, the hatred and the greed. When we overcome these, we bring peace and joy to ourselves and others.

When the lover is undeveloped, we become hostile and cruel. Without compassion, connection to life, we act in self interest or in the interest of one small group or nation. Without the warrior, we have no clear purpose in life. Our intention is weak or twisted. A weakened will or intention creates restlessness. The energy is moving aimlessly, seeking direction. Restless, we thoughtlessly move from experience to experience, grasping whatever appeals to the senses.

For me, the warrior is yet another face of the dancer. The warrior is the personification of the strength, courage and agility of the dancer. The warrior is strong in body and mind. She is animated by the inner poise and fearlessness that emerges through awakening the spiritual wisdom and energy, the power of love which brings forth the ability to care for oneself and the world, the inner power to live out our dreams. The warrior's power is the power of the will, a clear and strong intention that is aligned with the energy of the universe. When we live like warriors, we have a definite purpose, we are committed to that purpose with our whole body, mind and spirit. We manifest that purpose through clear and careful action. We are aware of the inner dance and we are in harmony with the dance of the universe.

"The warriors of olden times achieved their spiritual power by the most difficult self discipline, fasting and prayer, including the utter emptying of the heart of all earthly desires and the tuning of the inner ear to the whispers of the wilderness. . .this was the understanding of the Spirit of Being that manifests itself in all living things."[2]

The concept of the spiritual warrior,[3] one whose will is aligned with the harmony of the universe, is sorely needed in the world today. To continue to define will as a force over, is to continue to abuse power. As we grow into our humanness, we must deepen our understanding of the will. The development of will is a fundamental concept in the teachings of both Eastern and American Indians. I have learned three ways to align the will. First, the will is strengthened when we develop the abdominal muscles (see the section on physical exercises in this book). It is also strengthened through the power of the breath and through affirmation. One such affirmation, said on the inhalations, is "I infuse my body with the clear light of will." Exhale uncertainty. Inhale, saying, "My intention is clear and purposeful." Exhale fear. The third way of strengthening the will is by setting clear goals and then completing them. Choose something simple like "I will write two letters today," or, "I will water the plants." Then be sure to do it. Each time you set an intention and carry it out, you have created a full circle of energy and thereby strengthened your will. Inhale and make the intention. Exhale and take action. Inhale and affirm completion. Exhale.

As we continue to work in this manner, we begin to see the effects of being clear about what we are going to do and then doing it. This is learning the right use of will. When we know how to do this, we are able to make clear choices in life. I make a choice. I act. I see what happens. I understand the effect of my choice and action. I choose another action. I act and I observe its effect. Gradually we begin to see that we do have power, that we can make choices in our lives that will help to create and sustain positive situations. Something that happened when my children were younger illustrates this point. In our home, there were sometimes hassles around doing homework. While I was supportive of my children's feelings, I wanted them to understand that homework was their responsibility. If they chose to do the homework, there would be one result and, if they chose not to do it, there would be a different result. It wasn't about being good or bad or my trying to make them do something. It was clearly a choice and the choice was theirs to make.

Often we are not aware of what our intentions are, so the situations in which we find ourselves appear to be not of our choosing. As we deepen our self knowledge and come to understand what motivates us, we will better understand the outcome of our choices. Even when we find ourselves in a painful situation, we always have a choice about our attitude. As our understanding of a changing and interconnected universe deepens we find that cause and effect are connected. At this point, we become aware of our own repsonsibility. Power is energy that arises naturally from interdependent relationships. Each person has the power and each has the responsibility. The idea of victim is no longer useful. We have lived for many years in situations where there is an inequitable distribution of power. Understanding this, and coming out from under, is a process that takes courage, strength and perseverance. In no way does assigning responsibility to ourselves imply blame. Guilt, blame, humiliation, oppression are all limiting. The road to change may be a long one. Yet, there is a road and we have all begun to walk it.

The integration of the lover and the warrior, of compassion and action, is a lifelong commitment. The lover sees the commonality and shares equally. The warrior sees the particulars and takes action that will actualize what is good for all. As the lover we open our hearts; as the warrior we take clear aim. Together we direct our energy to build and nourish what is good for life. Today, more than ever before, we are called to integrate the many aspects of ourselves, to find the delicate and dynamic interplay of the opposites. Female and male, lover and warrior, compassion and action, are all aspects of a whole. Each contains the other. As we become open to seeing our greater being, we recognize that the sun and the moon exist within each of us. When we become as dynamic as our sun and as magnetic as our moon, we become the truly radiant stars that we are.

Each of the ten exercises in this chapter works with the process of integration. The first three suggest a particular archetype. These archetypes embody particular clusters of qualities. "Lovers and Warriors," and "Radiant Sun/Reflective Moon" both work with the integration of two archetypes which sometimes appear to be in conflict. The third exercise, "The Inner Artist," suggests a reason for integrating and expressing the creative life force. This is followed by two exercises which do not suggest an archetype; rather they create the space in which the many aspects of self can emerge and be brought into harmony. Then, there are three exercises which work with integration of the will. They are designed to help us understand our intention through the exploration of choice. The ninth exercise works with integration in the context of the grieving process. In this exercise and in "Celebrating Diversity" we come to recognize others as a part of ourselves. In the grieving exercise, we acknowledge the loved one we have lost as part of ourselves, realizing that they are alive in our hearts. "Celebrating Diversity," the last exercise in this series, brings the concept of integration to the social level where we recognize other cultures and other races as being connected to us, as part of ourselves, our family of humanity.

The process of integration enables us to see that the whole is greater than the sum of the parts. The world, at this time, is faced with many important decisions; choices that will determine whether we continue to exist as a planet. In order to keep ourselves from polarizing on issues of sex, class, race and religion, we have to come to a deep understanding of the concept of integration. Working with these exercises is a simple beginning. This work gives us a way of recognizing ourselves beyond the limits of personality so that we can begin to experience the profound awareness of the deep, enduring interrelationship of all of life.

Lovers and Warriors

In "Lovers and Warriors" we work with the energies of compassion and of action. It may be useful to work with the energy of one archetype at a time. Once you have a sense of each archetype, you can begin the work of balancing and integration. Most of us have a tendency to polarize different aspects of self. Working with an archetype is a way of working with the polarization. First we see the archetype as existing outside ourselves. As we communicate with it, we realize that it is actually a part of us. Through the act of visualizing the archetype, we awaken its qualities within ourselves. When we awaken the energy of lover and warrior and bring these energies into balance, we come to understand that the lover is also the warrior — one who acts with clear purpose and who is connected to all of life. And we understand that the warrior is a lover of life, whose movements are in balance.

> Bring your full attention to your breath as it enters and leaves your body. Inhale deeply, drawing in the energy of the Earth and letting it flow through you. As you exhale, let the energy return to the Earth. Keep your focus on your breath and on the full circle of Earth energy as it comes to you, moves through you, and returns to Earth.
>
> Imagine yourself in a beautiful place upon the Earth, a place where there is water, where the warmth of the sun is shining down upon you, a place where the air is clear and fresh. Imagine yourself filling with the energy of the sky and the Earth. Feel it flowing through your body, revitalizing you, healing you, energizing you. Breathe deeply and feel your connections with Mother Earth. Inhale the energy of Earth. Exhale and release doubt and fear. Inhale the energy of Earth and exhale

whatever is inhibiting your freedom in this moment.

Now, visualize a great and powerful warrior. See this warrior walking toward you. As the warrior approaches you, you can feel the strength and purpose within the warrior's movements. See the serenity and alertness in the warrior's face. Absorb the warrior's clarity of body and mind.

Spend some time with the warrior. Picture an incident in your life when the clarity of purpose and the purity of intention — the energy of the warrior — was wavering. Be with the warrior in this situation now, and transform the situation with the warrior's guidance.

When the experience feels complete, return with the warrior to the beautiful place in which you met. In this place, again visualize a being approaching you. This being is the lover. Envision the look of love and joy on the lover's face as you are recognized as the beloved. Feel the warm, gentle, loving energy that radiates from the lover. There are no barriers between you. Sense the unconditional love and total acceptance for who you are and where you are. Feel the power, the strength of compassion as this energy flows between you.

Spend some very important time with the lover. Bring to mind a time in your life when the energy of the lover, the warmth and power of kindness and love was wavering. Be with the lover in this situation, now, and transform the situation with the guidance of the lover.

When the experience feels complete, return with the lover to the place in which you met. As you sit, now with both the lover and the warrior, feel the strength of their compassion and grace. Observe the lover and the warrior as they join together in a dance of power, a dance of love, a dance of peace. As you watch, the lover and the warrior become one magnificent being, a union of compassion and action. This being bows to you and you begin to dance. As you dance, you feel power radiating from the being to you and from you to the being. As the dance continues, allow the being to slowly fade into light. Ab-

sorb the light into your body. As you awaken, know that
compassion and action are integrated within you. You are
the lover and you are the warrior.

Radiant Sun/Reflective Moon

This exercise is another opportunity to awaken and bring into balance qualities which we have polarized. The sun is not better than, or more important than, the moon. The sun and the moon are both part of a magnificent universe. Each is necessary and important; neither negates the other. "Radiant Sun/Reflective Moon" encourages us to play with the energies of sun and moon. You may want to obtain small representations of the sun and the moon to handle while working with this exercise or to place on your altar to demonstrate your intention of honoring and integrating these energies.

Imagine yourself seated firmly upon the Earth beside a clear lake. As you inhale, feel the energy of the Earth flowing up through your feet, into your legs, and up through your spine. Feel the Earth's energy deep inside you, deep within your spine. Each breath enables Earth energy to rise higher within your spine. Feel the Earth's energy flow up into your head and out the top so that it washes over your body and returns to the Earth. Continue to focus on your breathing, as the image or sensation of the Earth's energy flows through you, out the top of your head, washes over your body, and returns to the Earth.

See yourself reaching up into the sky. Feel as though your arms are outstretched and lifted up into the sky. Feel the warmth of the sun streaming down on your face. Feel the vibrant energy of the sun healing and revitalizing you. Inhale the energy of the sun; feel it move through you, melting your tension. Imagine the radiant energy of the sun streaming through every cell of your being. As the sun washes through you, it melts doubt, fear, anger, greed, lethargy. Feel the dynamic energy of the sun calling you to action. Awaken to the energy of the sun, its brilliant rays pulsing through your being. Imagine yourself dancing upon the Earth, the sun's rays streaming through you.

As the sky begins to turn a brilliant red/orange, and the sun moves closer to the horizon, feel yourself coming again to stillness. Watch as the setting sun paints the sky. And, as the sun sinks beneath the horizon, the moon begins to rise behind you.

Seated beneath the night sky, watch the moon beams dance upon the water. Feel the pull of the moon upon your body. Feel the magnetic energy of the moon as it draws any tensions from your body. Allow the moon to draw from you any fear or doubt, restlessness or anxiety. Feel the moon's reflective light as it shines down upon you.

And now, picture both the sun and the moon dancing in the sky. See a tiny sun falling down into your hands. Hold the sun in your right hand. See a tiny moon falling down into your hands. Hold the moon in your left hand. Begin to bounce the sun and the moon from one hand to the other. Toss them both into the air and catch the sun with your left hand and the moon with your right. Continue to toss the sun and the moon, catching them alternately in your left and right hands. Feel as though your are juggling the sun and the moon.

Feel the sun and all the qualities and energy you associate with the sun. Feel the moon and all the qualities and energy you associate with the moon. As you juggle these qualities, you are bringing into balance the energy of the sun and the moon within yourself. Feel what it is like to have both the radiance of the sun and the reflective power of the moon within you.

Now, hold both the sun and the moon quietly in your hands. Press both the sun and the moon to your heart. Feel the energies melting within you. Imagine that you are carrying the sun and the moon within your heart.

Awaken to the magnificent star-being that you are, dynamic as the sun and magnetic as the moon. Awaken to the star that you are.

The Inner Artist

Another face of the dancer is the artist, she who brings beauty and order to life. The artist is the deepening and actualization of the child's playful creativity. She is a weaver who is creating, with grace and precision, a colorful tapestry of life. The artist is sculptor, she who gives shape to vision and dream.

If we learned to think of ourselves as untalented or uncreative, or experienced ridicule as children, the artist within us may have been stifled. The artist within may have been silenced through too much pressure to perform, or the joy of our creative endeavors may have been stilled through fear of failure. If we think of artist only as one who creates with paint or clay, we may have a concept of artist that is limiting. The artist in us emerges each time we arrange flowers or integrate the many activities of our lives in a balanced way. She speaks through us when we have a particular flair for clothes or when we create loving, comfortable homes. The artist within is called forth in every deep-feeling response to people and to nature.

We can strengthen the artist through affirmations of our balance and creativity. She is also strengthened through journal writing, drawing dream images, playing with clay, and planting a garden. Bring an element of play to all of your activities. Experiment. Try writing or drawing with your weaker hand, for example, or with both hands at one time.

Visualization is a powerful tool for accessing the creative energy we all possess. "The Inner Artist" is a simple centering exercise, involving visualization, that can be done before beginning any creative endeavor. Remember that the word "artist" as we are using it here includes musician, writer, poet, sculptor, healer and more.

Inhale and allow your body to fill with clean, fresh air. Breathe deeply, all the way down into your coccyx. Exhale. Feel your abdominals gently contracting as the air is squeezed up and out of your body. Inhale and exhale. Allow the energy of the Earth to be drawn into your body. Let it nourish you, feed you. Exhale, and let it return to the Earth. Inhaling Earth, exhaling Earth. Always we are nourished and sustained by the Earth.

Now, imagine yourself moving through time and space, moving in and down and back and down, moving through time and space. Be aware of the light, streams of light, rivers of light. Moving through the light. Moving toward a great pool of light, a sea of light. This ocean of light is the creative energy of the universe. See it, feel it, immerse yourself in this vast pool of light. Allow yourself to be filled with the creative energy of the universe. This is the energy of life which we all share. We are all part of this vast sea of light, this creative energy of life. Be with this energy, be in this energy. Be creative energy.

Know that you have talents, capacities, gifts, abilities that lie within you. Know that you have the skills and talent of an artist. Allow that artist self, that creative self, to come forth and infuse your awareness. The artist, the shaper, the weaver, the dreamer. Let the vision of the artist awake. As that energy infuses you, feel your vision clearing, new perceptions arising. Spend some time in this awareness; be with the artist within. You may want to spend some time painting, drawing or sculpting. Allow the artist to draw from the sea of creativity, to become actualized within you.

Remain in touch with these feelings and perceptions, aware of the creative energy within you and awake.

Hall of Mirrors/Council of Selves

The next two exercises, "Hall of Mirrors" and "Council of Selves," can be used in conjunction with each other. In the first exercise, we have an opportunity to meet many different aspects of self. In the second exercise, we envision these aspects forming a council to advise and guide us. We listen to each speak in turn and then we present a challenging situation, for which we wish to have their guidance.

In our workshops we use these visualizations as part of a larger exercise. First people work in pairs, each making a life-size tracing of the other's body. Then we do the "Hall of Mirrors" visualization as a group. Immediately afterwards, the participants go to their pictures and draw inside of the outlines and around them the different images they uncovered during the visualization. When the drawings are complete, we play "Let's Visit the Museum." All the pictures are taped to the walls and people are asked to work in groups, talking about their creation to the other members of the group.It is very powerful to have a witness to the discovery of the various aspects of self. Other group members on the "museum tour" comment on the pictures, following certain guidelines: there is no analysis, only the expression of what one feels in observing the drawings. "I feel the power of the movement" or "I sense the conflict," are the kinds of responses that can be helpful. After the sharing, we gather together as one group again and, together, participate in the visualization, "Council of Selves," in which we recognize the voices existing within us and bring them together in resolution.

Hall of Mirrors

Let the coming and going of the breath bring you to a calm and centered space. Inhale and exhale. Feel the strength of the breath as it moves through you. Inhale and exhale.

Feel the energy of life flowing to you and through you. You are safely connected to the Earth, in deep relation to the Earth.

Imagine yourself in a circular room, a large hall. It is warmly lighted and the walls are covered with mirrors. Breathe deeply and face the first mirror. See reflected back to you an aspect of yourself. Look deeply into the eyes of the embodiment of this aspect.

As you continue to be aware of your breathing and your deep connection with the Earth, travel deep inside yourself. Imagine moving deep within until you come to a special place, a safe and clear space. You are surrounded by mirrors and as you turn around in the hall you know you are going to see, in each mirror, an aspect of yourself. It is from deep within this warm, safe, clear space that you approach the mirrors. Breathe deeply. Feel the serenity which always comes to you in this place.

Turn to your right and look into the next mirror. See reflected back to you another aspect of yourself. Look deeply into the eyes of this self and open to the understanding of yourself that is offered here.

Step in front of the third mirror. See reflected back to you yet another aspect of yourself. Again, look deeply into the eyes of this self, and continue this process of going from mirror to mirror, seeing the many aspects of yourself and accepting the understanding that is being given to you until you have experienced what each mirror holds for you.

Now, stand for a moment in the center of the hall and feel the many aspects of self within you. Give thanks for this knowledge and let the image of the hall of mirrors dissolve.

Focus again on your breathing. Breathe deeply and calmly for a few more minutes and, then, open your eyes.

Council of Selves

Return your focus to your breathing. Allow it to take you

deeper and deeper into yourself. Breathe deeply. Breathe in light and energy. Breathe out pain and confusion. Keep your focus on your breath.

Imagine that you are with all the aspects of your self that you met in the Hall of Mirrors. You are all together in a beautiful and safe space. Here, in this wonderful place, you can discover and explore all that you are. Here, in this place, meet with all the selves. See them sitting in a circle with you. Listen as each one speaks in turn. The Council of Selves is a most powerful council.

After all the aspects have spoken, ask them for their guidance concerning a particular issue that you are working with now. Allow each aspect to give advice and support. The Council of Selves is a most powerful council.

Remain in the Council circle for a few moments after you have heard in a very deep way all the advice offered to you by your many selves. Look at each aspect and thank him or her for their support.

When you are finished, allow the circle of selves to dissolve into light. Breathe in that light and feel the many dimensions of your being. Know that you have integrated the many aspects of self. Affirm, "I am whole. I am a balanced, centered, compassionate and energetic being."

The Council of Selves is a most powerful Council.

Let the affirmation fade and return from that space to this room. Open your eyes. You are filled with energy.

Recognizing Choice

"Recognizing Choice" is an exercise that will strengthen the will. We are not always aware of the many factors which determine our choices, so we sometimes feel as if we didn't choose, that a situation was forced upon us. As we look beneath the surface, we can learn to become aware of what we are choosing and how we go about making a choice. This knowledge allows us to begin to make the changes we desire in our lives. It is important to stress here that there is no blame. We are not blaming ourselves or anyone else. We are simply gathering facts, becoming more aware of what is happening. With this infomation, we are able to make clearer choices.

Inhale deeply and exhale completely. Each time you inhale, know that you are inhaling the clear light of will. Feel the power of will, the power of purpose and intention, infusing every cell, every atom, of your being. Inhale clarity of purpose. Exhale confusion and doubt. Inhale clear will and exhale confusion. Inhale courage and exhale fear. Inhale will and exhale confusion. Each time you inhale you are strengthening your will. Breathe in the clear light of will and let it infuse your whole being.

With every inhalation and exhalation, your will is strengthened, your purpose is strengthened. When you make intentions clear, and complete the tasks you set out to do, your will is strengthened. Each completed task strengthens the will. What you intend today builds your tomorrow. You are the creator of your life. You are the prophet of your future.

In every situation, you have a choice. You are able to recognize your choice. You are learning, now, to make your choices conscious. In every moment you can choose to act from love. In every situation you have a choice.

Visualize, now, a situation in which you wish to gain more clarity. From a space of open acceptance, see that situation and become aware of your part in its creation. See, feel and experience the situation. As you go deeper into this situation, let awareness arise. What feelings and thoughts led to the development of this situation? Ask yourself, "What is my part in its creation? What old patterns, habits or beliefs did I bring to this situation?"

Continue to be aware of your breathing and watch yourself in this situation without judgement. Allow yourself to receive the information the situation is offering you. Later, you can work with this information in whatever way you wish. For now, simply allow the information to come forth.

Ask yourself, "What situations have I been in in the past that are similar to this one? How is this situation similar to others I have been in and how is it different?" Spend enough time in the situation, asking these kinds of questions, to let important information come to you.

Now, see the situation changing. What do you want to happen? What do you want the situation to look like? What do you want your life to look like? Take time to explore choices other than the one(s) you originally made in this situation.

When you feel you have received enough information for now, allow the images to dissolve. Return your full attention to your breath. Breathe deeply and relax. Breathe in the clear light of will. Affirm the clarity of your intention. Then, open your eyes.

Expanding Alternatives

"Expanding Alternatives" continues our work with the will and with choice. In this exercise we choose a particular situation and we observe it from three different perspectives — that of the child, the adult and the elder. We learn to honor each of these perspectives and to become aware that each exists within us at all times. Acceptance of ourselves leads, naturally, to our acceptance of others. When we appreciate the child we discover within ourselves, we can better appreciate children in general and the child within everyone else. This exercise also strengthens the observer or witness within. We witness; we do not judge. We ask, "How would a child be in this situation? How would an elder react to this set of circumstances?" Exploring our choices in this way gives us an opportunity to expand our alternatives in every situation.

Inhale deeply and exhale completely. Inhale warmth and exhale clarity. Inhale warmth and exhale clarity. Let the light of love infuse every cell and every atom of your being. Let it bring you peace.

Now, picture yourself seated in a safe and comfortable place. Here you have the opportunity to safely and fearlessly look at a situation in your life which you find challenging. Bring this situation into your mind. Visualize yourself in the situation and allow your thoughts and feelings to emerge. Allow your doubts and confusion to arise. Seated here safely, there is no need for confusion or doubt to make you anxious. Let any questions you have about the situation come to the surface of your consciousness. Relax and spend a few minutes in the situation.

Inhale and breathe into you — the young, eager child. Let yourself awake as this child, alive and curious. This loving child, eager to explore, unafraid of taking risks, is awake within you now. She is observing the situation that you have presented. Take a few minutes to listen to the wisdom of your inner child.

Exhale, and release the child. Inhale, and breathe in the adult — the calm, centered adult who has participated successfully in numerous situations. The adult is awake within you now and she is observing this situation. She is sharing her perspective with you. Listen to her and receive the wisdom of the adult.

Exhale, and release the adult. Inhale, and breathe in the wise elder. This is the calm, compassionate elder with many years of experience and a deep understanding of self and others. This elder is with you now and she is sharing her wisdom with you. Receive the wisdom of the elder.

Now, exhale, and release the elder. Realize that old ways of perceiving may no longer be useful. These old ways can be released; let them leave you on the air of your exhalation. Know that the child, the adult and the elder live inside of you. With their perspectives, you will expand the range of your choices. With your expanded choices, you will create something of benefit to all of life, now and for many generations.

Examining Conflict

This is an exercise in which we witness our responses to conflict. It is an information-gathering exercise. In it, we are neither judging nor blaming. Conflict is an outcome of polarization; we feel split and the energies of each side battle the other. As we integrate, we see each part and its relationship to the whole, not apart from the whole.

Often, we find ourselves torn between one choice and another, one person and another, one idea and another. When we feel conflict, we weigh the benefits of one situation over the other, sometimes going from person to person to ask advice. One person tells us one thing, another has the opposite advice and a third says, "I can't tell you what to do." A new way to relate to conflict is to take time to explore the feeling. How is it experienced in the body? What are our responses to the *feeling* of conflict? Whenever we give our full attention to some behavior or attitude, it changes. Paying attention to the energy of conflict is a means of stilling the conflict. The feeling of conflict can be a habitual response. We may know what we want to do and not feel comfortable with our choice. In this case, our feeling of conflict protects us by preventing us from acting on our desire. If a part of us feels we continually need protection from the choices we want to make, we may use our feeling of conflict regularly to keep us from doing what another part of us knows won't be good for us.

Think of a conflict you experience in your life. It may be a conflict between inner archetypes (as between the warrior and the lover) or it may be a conflict between several different choices you could make. It could be a conflict between your affection for two people, or it could be another conflict altogether. Pick the conflict in your life that you would most like to learn something about at this time. "Examining Conflict" asks us first to explore the physical sensations of conflict within the body and then to look at our particular responses to conflict. The parts of the exercise may be done separately. You may want to spend one session observing the bodily sensations that arise when you are feeling conflict and another session looking at your behavioral responses to conflict.

> Focus on your breathing. Observe the coming and going of the breath — constant change, coming and going, in and out, inhale and exhale. Let the breath move through each part of your body. The breath, like your blood, circulates through the entire body. Releasing and relaxing. Releasing and relaxing.
>
> Imagine a quiet place in which you can explore the energy of conflict within yourself. Make the conflict you have chosen to explore become vivid in your mind's eye. See and feel yourself immersed in this conflict. Become aware of how you experience conflict within your body. Is the conflict localized in a particular place in your body? Do you feel it strongly in your jaw? The temples? The stomach? The shoulders? Where is conflict experienced in your body? How does your breath flow when you are engaged in conflict? Take your time and explore the sensations that arise in your body.
>
> Sit quietly and allow your responses to these questions to emerge from deep within you. Ask yourself, What is my general response to conflict? Am I so overwhelmed that I am unable to act? Do I act without thinking in an attempt to suppress my feelings? Do I use food, drugs or sex to escape the feelings of confusion that arise from conflict? Am I a pacifier? Am I an instigator? Do I try to deny that conflict exists? Sit with these questions and any others that may arise as you explore your reactions to conflict.
>
> When you have received enough information for this session, let your thoughts and feelings dissolve. Bring your attention back to your breath and watch it coming and going. Allow yourself to deepen, to relax and affirm, "I

am where I am supposed to be. I am aligned with the universal energy of life. I am able to reach the highest truth and live accordingly."

The Bonds of Love Are Never Broken

My father was buried very quickly after he died. The time we spent at the cemetery was very brief and, as I paused to make a small offering at the grave, I was asked by the funeral director to move on. The other people couldn't leave unless I did, he told me. At that time I was too sorrow-filled to say, "Tell them to go on," so I mutely left. American culture doesn't provide time for the integration of grief. We are allowed a few weeks and then everything is supposed to be "back to normal." The knowledge that the dead live on and still communicate with us is little talked about in this country. Fortunately, this is not the case in many other cultures. In the African world view, for example, the invisible world of spirit joins with human beings and the world of nature to form an organic reality. Luisah Teish tells us that, "Africans believe that those who go before us make us what we are. Through reverence for our ancestors we recognize our origins and ensure the spiritual and physical continuity of the human race."[4]

I worked with the following exercise just after my father died and it helped me to integrate those qualities that my father had reflected for me. While I was grieving his death I realized that he had provided me with a great sense of security. Because it had been many years since I had lived with my parents, I had not realized until he died that, in my psyche, he still represented protection for me. In this time of grieving, I realized that no matter where I was or what I was doing in my life, I had always expected my father to be sitting in his home office, always available for my call. As I explored the feelings that came up for me, I looked for ways to provide that sense of protection for myself.

In this exercise, which was inspired by some healing work I did with Boston healer, Julie Hobbs, we visualize the loved one we have lost and ask them to help us find ways of providing for ourselves what they have always provided for us. The bonds of love are never broken. Through my work on integrating some of his values, my father is still alive within me. I feel his advice coming to me from the spirit realm and, often, it seems clearer and stronger now that he is no longer limited by his cultural beliefs!

> Imagine a pyramid of light deep in the center of the Earth. Sense the pyramid generating spirals of light up from the center of the Earth. Breathe slowly and deeply, drawing the breath in through the soles of your feet. Imagine the energy flowing in through your feet and spiraling up through your body as you inhale. Know that this energy is always available to you.
>
> Inhale, as Earth energy rises up, moving through your body and out the top of your head like a white spray. Exhale and let this white spray wash over your body. Each time you inhale, receive the Earth energy. Each time you exhale, let the Earth energy flow out the top of your head, washing over you and draining back into the Earth. Be aware of the constant flow of energy from the Earth and to the Earth.
>
> Now, find yourself in a beautiful garden, calm and safe. Sit quietly and meditate in this garden. It is here that you will meet the one who has passed away. When you are ready, look up and see your loved one standing there with you. In silence, feel those qualities s/he reflected for you while they were living. Ask this person for help in developing those qualities within yourself. Be fully in this heart space and communicate with your loved one, holding yourself open to receive their love and guidance.
>
> When you are ready to leave, make a contract with your loved one, deciding how often you will meet. Thank her/ him and then watch as your loved one dissolves into light. Spend a few quiet moments in the garden, meditating, and then let the image of the garden dissolve. Open your eyes and know that the bonds of love are never broken.

Celebrating Diversity

This exercise, "Celebrating Diversity," is inspired by the teachings of the Sunray Meditation Society. It is a means for the individual to recognize herself as part of a planetary family. In "Celebrating Diversity" we imagine what it would be like to be a person of another race or background. We are, in a sense, attempting to walk in another's shoes. As we become more able to identify with others, we lessen the feelings of separation that create fear and hostility. It is a good idea to practice this exercise for several consecutive days, each day imagining yourself to be a person of a different culture. Deepen the practice until you can actually feel that everyone is a part of you and you are a part of everyone. The feeling will be strong; there will be no mistaking it. On a practical level, it will mean that you can no longer hide behind racial or cultural stereotypes. It will enable you to appreciate diversity, to recognize yourself in everyone you meet.

It is time to honor each other, to practice, as Luisah Teish suggests, "fidelity to the principle of reverence. Look around you. Is your dress made of Japanese silk? Yes? Then revere those ancestors. Having cornbread with dinner tonight? Recognize the work of Native Americans. Is that salsa music playing on the radio? If you just love that stuff, then salute your Latin ancestors.

"We can no longer afford to be tribal. There has already been too much physical and cultural exchange for that. . . . What we must now do is to turn to Mother Earth and salute Her for allowing us to live on Her body. We must feed Her, sing to Her and regard Her and all Her creations with loving reverence!"[5]

Imagine a light in the heart of the Earth. Sense its radiance as it pulsates upward from the Earth's center. Pulsating waves of light vibrate outward and upward from the Earth. As you inhale, receive the light of the Earth. Draw it up through your body. Feel your deep connection with the Earth. Feel your spine extending down into the heart of the Earth. Feel the nourishment that you are receiving from the Earth.

Now, as you sit here breathing, allow yourself to reflect on your life. Let images of your life flash before you. See your home, the people who surround you, your work, the daily routine of your life. Watch yourself go through a typical day. Let the images come quickly, without thought. Let the images arise as you consider your strengths and limitations.

Now return your attention to your breath. Breathe in and breathe out. Let your breath flow easily in and out of your body. Begin to imagine yourself to be a person of another race or culture. You may be the same sex or the other sex. You may have a different class background or it may be the same. Give yourself a few minutes to get used to your new body. Notice any changes in your facial structure, your skin color, your physical size, your hair. Notice what remains the same and what changes.

Breathe deeply and, as you exhale, allow yourself to imagine going through your day as this other person. What would be the same, if anything? What would be different? Notice your home, the people around you. Notice your partner or children, if any. Let the images come quickly and clearly. How do you get to work? Where do you work? See yourself on the job. How do people respond to your work? What is the same and what is different? Let the images arise quickly and easily as you observe your time after work, how you pursue your various interests. Who are your friends?

When you feel you have done enough for this session, allow the images to dissolve.

Now, see yourself as you are. Come back into your own body, with your own feelings, thoughts and sensations. When you are ready, open your eyes.

VIII
Changing Woman

It is Changing Woman who teaches the flow of life, the restlessness of
the sand as it flies with the wind, the wisdom of the ancient rocks that
never leave their home, the pleasure of the tiny sapling that has risen
through them. So it is into the House of the Changing Woman that each
young girl enters, as her blood begins to flow with the moon, as she
passes into womanhood.

It is Changing Woman who teaches the cycles, the constant round of hot
and cold, of birth and dying, of youth and aging, of seedling to corn,
of corn to seedling kernel, of day to night, of night to day,
of waxing moon to waning moon — and thus She gave the sacred songs
to ease all in their passage.

It is to Changing Woman that we look as we search
for the wisdom of life. While some may believe they can defy
Changing Woman's patterns to make their own,
wise people know that this cannot be done,
for to try to change the ways of Changing Woman,
is to destroy all life. Those who understand the ways
of Changing Woman, forever walk The Trail of Beauty.

—Navaho Creation Story.[1]

Where there is a woman there is power. A woman's power is special. A woman's power is unique. A woman is the Full Circle. A woman's power is to create. A woman's power is to nurture. A woman's power is to heal. A woman's power is to transform. A woman's power is both dark and light. A woman knows that nothing can be born without darkness and nothing can come to fruition without light.

Woman's body is both a vessel for and a metaphor of transformation. Ancient peoples of all cultures, awed by the processes of birth, lactation and menstruation, called them "Women's Mysteries." A mystery is a secret, an unseen act of transformation. It is awesome and cannot be understood or interpreted by the intellect alone.

Every creative act is an act of birth. We birth children of the flesh and children of the mind. We give birth to every thought we hold. The mystery of lactation can be seen as a metaphor for the power to choose which ideas and forms we will nourish. How we make choices, set priorities, the values we hold, and to what we devote our love, energy and resources, are all indications of the ways we nurture.

In my life the physical acts of birthing, lactating and mothering have been an incredible means for sourcing my power. While these are not choices every woman would make, or should make, they are ones which have had an enormous impact on every aspect of my life. The joys and sorrows of motherhood have provided me with a wealth of knowledge and resources. It is my path of power and my spiritual practice. Whether or not we choose motherhood, we need to bring a fresh perspective to the experience of mothering. The authors of *Women's Ways of Knowing* clarify for us the knowledge gained through this process. "By pleasing others we become sensitized to the needs and moods of other people. Placating family members and close friends taught us much about negotiation and groups. Financial and organizational skills were learned through household management. Raising our children taught us about growth, illness and health."[2]

Tsultrim Allione affirms the power of motherhood when she states, "The path of the mother should be given its deserved value as a sacred and powerful spiritual path."³ Tsultrim, a teacher and herself a mother, says that male spiritual teachers don't seem to address this subject. A mother, too, can be a spiritual warrior. Mothering is a way of developing patience, strength and endurance. Tsultrim sees endless possibilities for recognizing motherhood as a spiritual path. Motherhood is a constant testing of the Buddhist Bodhisattva Vow to save all sentient beings before ourselves. It is certainly a practice of selflessness. We can bring a sacred sense to our homes and to the preparation of food. These are divine acts. To see the one-value, the divine essence of all things, whether diapers or roses, is a worthy challenge.

What is needed to save the world is a mother's touch. When we are infants we are completely helpless; we survive only because someone is willing to put their needs second to ours. Now humankind needs to mother itself in order to survive. We need to learn to nurture ourselves, each other and the Earth herself. Whether or not we physically give birth, we are all mothers. The power to love, to sense connection, to nurture, to feel and act with compassion, is the power needed to sustain the world.

Ancient cultures revered the changing woman, the creator of all life. This reverence for the interconnectedness of life was often demonstrated through the act of ritual. Each culture had its rituals to celebrate important changes in people's lives. Births, coming of age, new discoveries, strong dreams, conflicts resolved, unions, losses and deaths were all ritualized.Today, we have forgotten the power of ritual. We associate it with superstition or with the religion we were taught as children, a religion that may no longer hold meaning for us. There are few, if any, living rituals to mark the important passages in our lives. Probably the most widespread ritual in our culture today is that of sending cards. There are cards to mark every occasion. I think beneath the hurriedness and commericalism of this ritual is the soul's longing to positively note important life changes.

In my life, I have found the act of ritual to be a source of strength and power. It enables me to clarify my intentions, concretize inner events, mark important changes and acknowledge the interconnectedness of all life. Every ritual, from the simplest lighting of a candle to the most involved and lengthy ceremony, shares in common several stages. There is the planning of the ritual and the gathering of the materials, as well as the inner preparation which may include meditation, fasting, bathing or some other purification, and then the performing of the ritual itself.

When planning a ritual your intention is most important. Ask yourself why you want to have a ritual. What do you want its effect to be? Is the purpose of this ritual in harmony with the energy of the universe? Is it being done for the greatest good for all? Once your intention is clear, then the inner preparation begins.

The planning of the ritual includes deciding which occasion to ritualize, picking the date and the time, choosing between a solitary ritual and a group ritual. If you decide to have a group ritual, you must decide whom to invite. After these things are settled, the objects to be used in the ritual are gathered. This stage may include the setting up of an altar where each of the elements are represented — a candle for fire, a bowl of water, incense for air, a stone or salt for the Earth. These and other objects symbolizing transformation are appropriate. You may want to choose food and musical instruments for use in the ritual. Include in the ritual whatever objects your heart is drawn to.

People often wear special clothes for rituals. When they wear this clothing only for rituals, a special energy builds up in the clothing itself. In rituals of self-blessing, you may want to use special water, such as rose water. Or you may want to choose a favorite oil for anointing. You may want to smudge yourself by passing the smoke from burning cedar and sage around your body.

If you decide to do a ritual for several days in a row, you may want to make an altar where you can keep a votive candle burning as a reminder that your prayer and your energy is being sent continuously. Take care with this candle so as not to start a fire. Place it in a private place so that the energy and interest of others will not diffuse the strength of your rituals and affirmations.

The rituals I have included here are simply suggestions. As you read and perform them, you will begin to get a feel for the creation of ritual and eventually, you will want to create your own rituals.

Calling Your Unborn Child

This ritual can be performed by a woman who wants to have a child. It is a very simple ritual that can be done at any time. The old ones say that the time of the full moon is the time for granting wishes so it is especially good to do this ritual at that time. Psychic and intuitive power is also particularly strong at the time of the full moon. You may perform this ritual alone or with a partner. Its purpose is to open your heart and call the soul that would enter through you.

As with every ritual it is important that you clarify your intention before you begin. Courageously consider the reasons you want to have a child. In this era there is much confusion about ownership and domination. We may want children in order to have someone of our own (that is, someone to own), or we may want someone to carry on our name, or to accomplish the things we were unable to accomplish in our own lives. In a culture where happiness is often defined in terms of acquisitions, it is very important to be sure of our reasons for wanting to have a child.

We have made advances in reproductive technology at an alarming rate and now we must carefully consider whether every possibility for childbirth available to us has to become an actuality. We must remember that everything in the universe is connected and we are not always aware in the moment of what the long range effects of our actions will be. For this reason, Native Americans teach us to "consider all actions unto seven generations."

It is an honor to become a parent. A mother is the doorway through which we gain entrance into this world. I have always loved the words of Kahlil Gibran in *The Prophet:*

Your children are not your children
They are the sons and daughters of life's
longing for itself
They come through you but they are not
from you
And though they are with you
They belong not to you
You can give them your love
but not your thoughts
They have their own thoughts
You can house their bodies
but not their souls
You can strive to be like them
But you cannot make them just like you.

Prepare for this ritual by cleaning the space in which it will be performed. Prepare your mind by setting aside your doubts and fears. Burn some cedar and sage to clear the air and set up an altar with objects symbolizing what you wish to provide for the child. Now, leave this space and further prepare by taking a bath by candlelight. Dress carefully for the ritual and return to the space in which it is to be performed.

Anoint yourself according to your spiritual practice. You may use water, oil or smudge. Light candles and sit in front of your altar. Bring your full attention to your breathing for a few minutes until you feel calm and centered.

Feel your heart opening to the universe. As it opens, call to your child with your heart and mind. Speak of your readiness and desire to care for and nourish another. State your intention clearly. Ask the soul whose vibration is most in harmony with your vibration, who would benefit from your loving guidance, to come to you. Use whatever words feel right to you. You might say, "I open my heart to a child. I ask the child who would benefit most from my (our) loving care to come. I (we) are ready for you." Feel your contact with this soul and continue to communicate, speaking of your preparation, your readiness to receive a child and whatever else you feel called to say.

When you feel finished, snuff the candles and sit in the dark. Give thanks to the universe and affirm your relationship to its beauty and order. When the ritual is complete, leave the space.

When You Cannot Carry the Child

A young friend once asked me to be with her when she was having an abortion. Although she doesn't practice rituals or meditate, she spent many sleepless hours the night before the abortion talking to the child-soul, speaking of her love for the child, saying that, at this time, she was unable to have a child and asking for forgiveness. It was this young woman's experience that inspired the creation of this ritual.

No woman should be forced to carry a child she is unable to care for. Human life is very, very precious and we must consider the psychic and emotional pain of both the mother and the child-soul. The objective of this ritual is to heal the pain of both. It may be performed at any time, either prior to an abortion or after one. It can be done many years after an abortion; the time is not important here. What is important is the heart's opening and the communication between the souls.

Prepare for this ritual by clearing a space in a room where you can make an altar. Alternatively, you can prepare a space just in your heart. You may want to light a candle and make a smoke offering by burning incense or sage.

Breathe deeply and come to a calm space. Focus your awareness on your breathing for a few minutes and, when you feel ready, open your heart to the life beginning within you or to the child-soul that was once a part of you. Share your deep feelings. Speak of your love and concern for the child-soul. Tell of your inability to bring a child into the world at this time. Share from the deepest place in your heart and ask forgiveness of the child-soul. Be gentle with yourself and forgive yourself. Take time to make peace with yourself and with the child-soul. You may want to include the "Self-Forgiveness" exercise as part of this ritual.

When you feel the ritual is complete, snuff the candle and sit for a few moments in darkness. Then, leave the space.

You can repeat this ritual as often as you feel is necessary for the healing to be complete.

Heart to Heart Communication

In this ritual a pregnant woman communicates with her unborn child. Mothers, of course, are doing this all the time during pregnancy. With the deep, intimate contact of mother and child, it is not only food and blood that is shared. The child in the womb may not be aware of all the specific incidents in our lives but the emotional tone of the life comes through. When I was a child in my mother's womb, I could feel her deep love and desire for me. I knew I was very much wanted. I also felt her deep sorrow at the death of her mother which had occurred several months before my birth. Because of this experience, I felt for many years that the loss of one's mother was the deepest sorrow.

This ritual makes the heart to heart communication between the mother and child more conscious. Some of my friends have given to their child the name they received while performing this ritual. It is a good idea to do this ritual frequently during pregnancy.

The preparation for this ritual is simple. Choose a time each day or every few days to spend communicating with your unborn child. You may want to sit in front of your altar while doing this and you may want to place on the altar some special piece of cloth or jewelry that you intend to give your child. You may find it very helpful to keep a record of these communications in a journal.

Focus your attention on your breathing. Imagine sending your breath into each part of your body until you become relaxed and centered. As you inhale, draw the energy of the Earth, the mother of us all, into your body and into your child's body. Let the earth energy move through you. Picture the warm sun above your head. Breathe in the healing light of the sun.

Now, see yourself floating in a warm pool. Feel the water surrounding you. As you float, focus your mind and heart on the life that is floating inside of you. Continue to focus until you are aware of an energy exchange. If you do not feel the exchange of energy, imagine it.

This soul, this being, has a special purpose. This soul who will come through you has unique gifts to share with the world. Feel your relationship to this new life. Affirm your willingness to nurture this soul so that it can develop and fulfill its greatest potential. Spend some special time communicating heart to heart with this being. Listen to the heart of the child. Open to and honor this communication. You may want to ask particular questions, such as "Who are you? What do I need to know about you? How can I best care for you?"

When you feel that the communication is complete for this time, wish the child well and give thanks for its presence. Again, see yourself floating peacefully in the water. Then, see yourself climbing out of the water and, in your imagination, allow the sun to dry you.

Entering the House of Changing Woman

This is a woman's ritual to honor a young girl who is entering the "house of changing woman." Creating rituals to celebrate menstruation is an act of power. It is a remembering and a renewing of the ancient power of woman. These rituals can be simple ones, shared only by mother and daughter or they can include friends of both mother and daughter. I have participated in similar rituals for my friends' daughters for many years.

The preparation for this ritual begins with your talking with your daughter about your desire to ritualize this important event. If your daughter feels comfortable with the idea of a ritual, share with her from your heart your feelings about becoming a woman. Encourage her to share her feelings with you and be receptive to them. Talk about the power to give birth, not only to physical children but to all we create. Both of you may wish to explore how other friends feel about menstruation.

You may also want to look together at how people in other cultures, both ancient and modern, have celebrated the moon time. Many Native American cultures viewed the moon time as the time of woman's greatest power. They understood the release of unneeded blood and tissue from a woman's body as a release of energy. This energy was recycled; as the blood returned to the Earth, old thoughts and feelings returned also to the Earth, to become fertilizer for new patterns of thought and action. The bleeding woman would stop her usual activities and spend the days of her period in prayer and meditation. She prayed for her whole community, that they might release the old and give birth to the new.[4]

Together, mother and daughter can explore ancient rituals and discover their relevance for today. We all need a time for contemplation, a time to reflect, to see what within us needs release. How fortunate woman is to have a special reminder of these needs. Her body during menstruation is showing her the power of release. Each month we can pray for all our relatives and friends. We can pray that they will be able to release what they no longer need and create for themselves what is now most appropriate. We can share with our daughters the importance of having a time to be quiet, to rest from our usual activities. Menstruation is a time of renewal as well as of release. We are renewed so that we can return, clearer and stronger, to loved ones. It is a good time for the whole family. From a ritual of this kind we learn to respect one another and to respect the cycles of life.

Together with your daughter decide the day on which this ritual will take place and agree on whom you will invite. You will want to think together of symbols that can represent woman's power during the ritual. You may wish to include special food or music. You might want to plan with your friends to bring small gifts for your daughter.

Your daughter may want to plan some of the ritual with you and allow some of it to be a surprise to her. There is mystery and excitement in this passage from childhood to womanhood.

> On the day of the ritual, prepare a space to honor your daughter. Ask your daughter to build an altar and make whatever other preparations you have agreed upon. She may want to have her friends help her with some of the preparations. When everything has been arranged, the daughter prepares herself by taking a special bath. As she rests in water and watches the flowers she has placed in the bath water float on the surface, she has time to reflect on the meaning of this passage. She then dresses in the clothes she has chosen for this ritual.
>
> The ritual begins with all participants, except the mother and daughter, sitting silently in a circle, breathing together and centering themselves. When it is time for the mother and daughter to enter, the members of the circle chant or sing, perhaps calling out "Woman, enter woman time,

woman enter," or some other chant that you make up yourself.

When the mother hears the chanting, she brings the daughter into the circle as the members of the circle speak or sing their welcome. Now, the mother and the other older women can talk aloud about this special time and share their individual expressions of welcome with the daughter. Each may speak in turn and bless the daughter with a gift. As the daughter receives each gift, she places it on or near the altar as a way of honoring it. When the gifting is complete, the daughter may wish to share her feelings of thanks.

Now, mother and daughter join hands with the other members of the circle, and the entire group sits together for singing, chanting, or silent meditation. After this, red yarn is passed from woman to woman, each wrapping it around her wrist until all the women are joined together with this powerful symbol. You may want to sing while the joining is going on. When the joining feels complete, each woman breaks the yarn and saves a small piece to take with her as a memento of the ceremony.

Now the circle is opened, food is shared, and all participants continue to enjoy the celebration.

Cave Dreamers

In many Native American traditions, the time of the blood is a time of power. At the time of her blood, a woman withdraws from her regular duties and spends her time praying and meditating for her people. The energy of the prayer, the opening of the heart to the universal wisdom, is honored as women's special duty during this time. The release of unneeded blood and tissue from her body is seen as a natural "sweat," a transformation and release of energy. Working with the natural rhythm of the bodily cycle, the woman is released from any limiting thought forms and, symbolically, her people are simultaneously released. The energy of limiting thought forms, like the blood, returns to the Earth to be recycled. In the now empty womb, new forms can be created to bring good for the whole circle of life. Some Native American peoples built menstrual huts where the bleeding women sat together. While some tribes did not have this practice, it is likely that all peoples, of whatever nation, at one time revered the woman's bleeding time as a time of power.

In a time when women's power, in general, is denigrated, the power of the blood has been forgotten. Today, the time of bleeding is seen as a time of weakness. Menstrual blood is often considered to be smelly and unclean. We are taught to act as though nothing is changing, nothing is happening during the time of our bleeding. This denial of a natural bodily function, in my opinion, is the cause of the cramping and other premenstrual symptoms many women experience. We need to look with fresh vision on this cycle and begin again to revere its connection to the cycles of universal change. We need to create space in our lives to welcome the time of bleeding as a time of turning inward. We need to remember that this time is a time of power for us, the power of creation is manifested in it. We have the power to create ideas, images, thoughts, new ways of living and, of course, the power to give birth to children. Everything that has ever been born has had a mother.

In this exercise, "Cave Dreamers," we can connect with the ancient source of women's knowledge, with the ancient source of women's sacred power. As we affirm the time of the blood and make space for it in our lives, the wisdom it provides can manifest in our daily reality. In "Cave Dreamers" we acknowledge the power of the dream, the place where visions arise. We affirm our willingness to bring into physical reality the dream of peace and well-being for the whole Earth.

> Breathing in and breathing out. Breathing, drifting, traveling on the breath. Traveling back through time and space, traveling back to another time, back to the cave of your being.
>
> Visualize yourself walking in a mountainous area. Know that hidden somewhere in these mountains is a cave. Move, quietly and gracefully, through these mountains, knowing that you are guided by some long ago instinct. Feel yourself drawn toward the cave of your being.
>
> Now, see yourself at the entrance to the cave. You have to crawl through a damp and narrow space as you enter it. Light the torch you have carried with you and continue to crawl deep into the recesses of this cave. You move confidently through the passageways until you come to an open space, large enough for you to stand and walk around. As your torchlight falls on different parts of the walls you notice bits of minerals, shining. You see, faintly, the outlines of drawings.
>
> You know this is the cave of the dreamers and we are the women who dream. This is the cave of the dreamers who dream sweet dreams, wise dreams, dreams of clear purpose, dreams of compassion and strength. We are women of the cave. We are the women who dream. When our minds are clear and our hearts are open, the dreams are strong.
>
> Remember, we were taken to this cave at the time of

our first blood. We were led to this cave by our grand-mothers who shared with us here the secret of the cave, the secret of women dreaming. Grandmother whispered in a voice soft, yet strong, "This is the place for women of our blood, this is the place of our power. This is the place for our dreams, the power of dreams that will last when civilizations pass. This is the place of our power. In this cave you link with the circle, the circle of women joined. Women who love life, who preserve life, who nourish and sustain life. This is the cave of our dreams."

Grandmother showed us how to make the paints and draw the pictures on the walls of this cave, the pictures that will carry the energy of the dream, which will make the dream come true. Look closely now. Walk with your torch right up to the wall of the cave and see the deep secrets of woman's heart. See the secrets of life everlasting, secrets of cycles ever-changing and renewing. See the pictures women, generation after generation, have painted on the walls of the cave.

It is you who are here now. You stand alone, confidently, ready to create your own pictures, ready to paint your own pictures on the cave walls. It is here that you will dream strong dreams. Begin, now, to make your paints. Begin to paint your pictures on these walls. Quietly, with concentration, you paint your dreams.

When the dreaming and drawing feels complete, leave the sacred chamber. Crawl back through the narrow tunnel, back into the sunlight. Know that you can return to the cave each month, or whenever solitude calls, whenever your dreams and prayers are for the well-being of all life.

Celebrating Menopause

Menopause, like menarche in a culture that denies women, is not honored. We can change this by creating our own rituals and celebrations for menopause. For women who have been busy with children and family duties, menopause is a time to extend skills and knowledge to a larger community. The time of menopause is a time when duties change. It is a deepening for all of us, whether we have worked in the home, outside of it, or both. Like all passages, our feelings about menopause may be mixed. There may be sorrow over things left undone, opportunities denied. There may be joy as we settle into the new wisdom that is coming to us at this time. A celebration ritual is a time to honor all the emotions and to affirm our inner power to create and to change. In an era when menopause is viewed as a drying up, a time of decline, a time to be feared, it is essential that women come to a new awareness. I encourage you to join with your women friends to celebrate the great event of menopause. Celebrating this event with men as well would give all the opportunity to honor this important passage in our lives and to recognize menopause as a time of deepening power and wisdom.

The following may be done as a visualization or it may become part of a larger ritual that you plan and prepare with your friends.

> Focus on your breathing and let your breath deepen and relax you. Focus only on your breath so that thoughts become simple. And, then, thoughts become silent.
>
> When you feel yourself centered, see yourself outside in a beautiful place. The sun is shining brightly, the sky is deep, deep blue with only a few fluffy white clouds in it. The wind plays with the cloud shapes, dances

through the clouds, reforming and reshaping them. Drink in the vibrant beauty of your special place — the flowers, the trees, the rich earth. Listen to the sound of the birds singing in the trees. Become aware of nature, alive, pulsing all around you. This is your special place.

Move freely upon the Earth, feel her pulsing and vibrating beneath your feet. Know that the Earth's energy is spiraling up through your feet and legs, and dancing through your body. Feel your most deep and satisfying connections with the Earth. Let your body move — slow, gentle stretching at first. Now, begin to quicken your step. See yourself dancing freely upon the Earth. Let the Earth sing to you as you dance with her, for her. Honor the Earth below your dancing feet, and honor the warmth of the sun's healing rays above you. Dance free.

As you dance round and round, as you turn, see yourself as a young girl, dancing, turning, spiraling. See that young girl at the time of her first moon. Dancing and turning, honor the gift of that time. You have the power to release any pain and sadness. Honor the gift of that time.

Dancing round and round, dancing through your life. See a young woman, mother of her thoughts, maybe mother of children. Mother of her own life. See your changing body. See your changing life. You have the power to transform any pain or sadness. Honor the gift of your life.

Dancing, dancing, dancing patterns of light as you move through your life. Honor the cycles, honor the seasons. You have the courage to transform the pain of the past. You have the courage to bring forth a new time. Receive the gift of your life.

Aware of the mystery, aware of life ever-changing, greet this new phase of your life. Arms up, swirling and dancing, welcoming the new phase in the cycle of life. Moving through life's changes. Changing patterns. Renewing. Healing. Dancing through your life. Coming fully into the body, into your woman wisdom. Honoring yourself.

Honoring your spirit, honoring your life.

Be alive. Be vibrant. Receive the gift of this time. This gift is for you. This gift is for all people. This is the gift of the ending of the moon cycle. Receive the gift of this time.

Now, gently, gradually, begin to let the dance come to stillness. Breathe deeply. Sense the Earth; sense yourself on the Earth. Ever aware of the circle of life. Ever aware of the mystery of life. Touch the Earth. Reach to the sky. Be one with the circle of life.

Motherlines

Time exists as an organizing function of the mind, helping us to handle the details of our daily lives. In the greater scheme of the cosmos, there is no absolute time. The theory of relativity from modern physics shows that space and time are not separate; they are intimately connected and, together, form something called "space/time." There is no universal flow of time. Space and time are concepts used to describe reality; they are not reality.

Who we are is something composed of both "past" and "future." We exist in the ever-changing present moment. One of the ways to sense this movement, to feel these connections is to connect with the wisdom of our ancestors. This exercise, "Motherlines," can help both women and men to recall the mother wisdom and to activate it, now, so that the Earth may continue to survive. Mother wisdom does not negate father wisdom; it includes father wisdom. Women and men can use this same exercise to trace fatherlines and to get in touch with father wisdom.

We are alive today because of the caring and compassion of mother. She was there to feed us when we were helpless. Yet, mothering is not limited to caring for infants; we all need mothering. It is this care and concern which enables us all to survive. We need to awaken the power of creation and nurturance in all beings. Families, cultures, nations were all created through people's efforts to share and care for each other. Today, the natural flow of life, the natural exchange of energy has been reduced, through fear, to a bargain and exchange paradigm of relationship. Now we are full of expectations, demands, disappointments and feelings of oppression. We must recall the generosity we have experienced in the past. Perhaps some of the images we call forth in "Motherlines" will be ones of pain and sadness, even despair. Some will be images of strength and power. We must call upon our courage to reach down beneath the pain to the constant source of nourishment that exists within each of us. We must be able to see what has been given without being fooled by the sometimes twisted way in which it was passed to us. This is a great gift. We take a risk opening to these feelings. We must allow our hearts to break again and again, so that we can truly experience joy.

Sometimes the pain we have felt causes us to negate a whole experience so that we miss the kernel of truth or goodness that was present for us. Unresolved issues from the past cloud our ability to be completely present. When we can fully open to the past, accept it, integrate it into our lives, we are brought fully into the present. "Motherlines" is a journey into resources as human beings. We all come from a long lineage of mother wisdom.

> Sink, sink, sink deep into the breath. Feel your whole consciousness drawn into the process of breathing. Be fully present with the breath. Breathe deeply. Feel as though the energy of the Earth is being drawn up through your feet as you inhale. Feel this energy rising up through your body and out into the sky as you exhale. Inhale, and feel the energy of the stars being drawn into your head. Exhale, and feel it flowing down in the Earth. Become one with the breath, one with the Earth, one with the sky. Sink deep into the breath.
>
> Come to the place where the dream begins, come to the place of the dreams. The dream space is a space of light. Come to the light and the dream. Here, in the dream, meet your mother. This is the time to cast off any fear, any anger, any pain that you may feel when you feel mother. Here, in the light, meet your mother with love and clarity. Share, in this dream space, your mother's dreams. Hear her wisdom. Sense the seed of wisdom she has carried through this life. Here, in the light, receive the gift of your mother.
>
> Here, in the dream space, moving through the light,

meet your grandmothers. Greet your grandmothers and receive from them the knowledge that they bring you. Receive their gift. Let them speak to you. Feel the wisdom of the grandmothers.

Here, in the dream space, meet your great-grandmothers. Greet them and know that they have come to share with you their wisdom, to pass on to you the knowledge they have carried through the ages. Let them speak to you. Receive their gift.

Here, in the light, in the dream space, move through the motherlines. Meet the long lineage of women, the lineage of your birth. Follow the motherlines, traveling through space/time, tracing the motherlines. Receive the wisdom of women, the wisdom of ages past. Honor the motherlines. Move through the years, centuries, ages past. Trace the motherlines.

When the experience feels complete for this session, awaken with the knowledge of the mother deep within you. Awaken fully to present.

Afterword

It has been my good fortune to have the opportunity to travel throughout the United States, Canada and Great Britain teaching and sharing. In this last year Shuli and I have worked in groups primarily with the exercises, meditations and rituals from this book and, in this sharing, we have discovered again and again the power of simplicity. The message we bring is not new. We offer, simply, another opportunity to hear and to practice.

In recent years the study of psychic phenomena has become quite popular. While this turn of events is very exciting to me, I am also aware of the challenge it presents to all of us. Can we open to this information and, at the same time, remain grounded? We can get lost in space. When calling in the spirits, it is good to have someone home to welcome them! So our practice is very simple. Sometimes it is even boring — it is just to sit and watch the crazy antics of mind. Yet, it is this sitting that loosens the habits of mind so that wisdom can come through.

The opportunity to share, to sit, to celebrate with many people is an honor and a joy. Each circle sends its ripples out over the whole planet. We are happy to be a part of this awakening. We share this book with you. May you feel the inner dance. May the music of this dance of life, this dance of love, resound throughout the planet.

Footnotes

Chapter I. How to Use this Book

1. *Starhawk, The Spiral Dance: A Rebirth of the Ancient Religion of the Great Goddess*, Harper and Row, New York, 1979.

Chapter II. Awakening the Dancer

1. I am indebted to Tsultrim Allione, author of Women of Wisdom, for her elaboration of Buddhist thought.
2. Dhyani Ywahoo, Spiritual Director of the Sunray Meditation Society, P.O. Box 308, Bristol, VT.
3. Stephen Levine is a psychologist who writes on, among other things, issues surrounding death and dying
4. Stephen Levine, *A Gradual Awakening*, Doubleday Anchor Books, New York, 1979.

Chapter III. Foundations

1. In actuality, there are no fixed, rigid and separate levels. I am using this language to facilitate communication in bringing us from an "either/or" understanding to a "both/and" understanding. Many things happen simultaneously.
2. One estimate, reported by Dr. Larry Dossey, author of *Space, Time and Medicine*, tells us that each of our inhalations contains at least one atom breathed by every person on the Earth for the last four weeks. This is due to the thorough mixing of the Earth's atmosphere.
3. Sunray Meditation Society, founded and directed by Dhyani Ywahoo of the traditional Etawa band of the Eastern Tsalagi (Cherokee) Nation is an international spiritual society dedicated to world peace. The address for Sunray is P.O. Box 308, Bristol, VT.
4. This section on the chakras was written in collaboration with Bonnie Novakov-Lawlor.
5. This section was also written in collaboration with Bonnie Novakov-Lawlor.

Chapter V. Loving, Forgiving, Releasing

1. John Moyne and Coleman Barks, *Versions of Rumi*, Threshold Books, 1984.
2. Barbara Walker, *Women's Encyclopedia of Myths and Secrets*, Harper and Row, San Francisco, 1983.
3. Pat Rodegast and Judith Stanton (compilers), *Emmanuel's Book*, Some Friends of Emmanuel, New York, 1985.
4. You may envision a child of a different age at this time, or you may decide to envision your child self at different ages, starting with the age you were at your earliest memory and working upward in small increments. You

may envision children of different ages in the same session or you may decide to choose a particular age and work with it throughout an entire sitting, choosing the same or another age for other sessions.

Chapter VI. Transformation

1. Jane Wagner, *The Search for Signs of Life in the Intelligent Universe*, Harper and Row, San Francisco,1986.

Chapter VII. Integration

1. Feminist writer, Marcia Black, shared with me her interpretation of this ancient teaching.
2. William Willoya and Vinson Brown, *Warriors of the Rainbow*, Naturegraph Publishers, Happy Camp, California, 1962.
3. My work with Dhyani Ywahoo has been instrumental in my learning to understand the way of the warrior.
4. Luisah Teish, *Jambalaya: The Natural Woman's Book of Personal Charms and Practical Rituals*, Harper and Row, New York, 1985.
5. Ibid.

Chapter VIII. Changing Woman

1. From Merlin Stone's *Ancient Mirrors of Womanhood*, Beacon Press, 1984.
2. Belenky, et. al., *Women's Ways of Knowing*, Basic Books, New York, 1986.
3. Tsultrim Allione, *Women of Wisdom*, Routledge & Kegan Paul, Boston, 1984.
4. For a deeper exploration of how Native Americans viewed the sacred time of menstruation, see *The Sacred Hoop* by Paula Gunn Allen, Beacon Press, 1986.

Bibliography

Paula Gunn Allen, *The Sacred Hoop: Recovering the Feminine in American Indian Traditions*, Beacon Press, Boston, 1986.

Tsultrim Allione, *Women of Wisdom*, Routledge and Kegan Paul, Boston, 1984.

Mary Field Belenky, et al., *Women's Ways of Knowing: The Development of Self, Voice and Mind,* Basic Books, New York, 1986.

Larry Dossey, *Space, Time and Medicine*, Shambhala, Boston, 1982.

Kahlil Gibran, *The Prophet,* Random House, New York, 1923.

Eliana Gil, *Outgrowing the Pain: A Book for and About Adults Abused as Children*, Launch Press, Calif. 1983

Stephen Levine, *A Gradual Awakening*, Doubleday Anchor Books, New York, 1979.

John Moynes and Coleman Barks, *Open Secret Versions of Rumi*, Threshold Books, Vermont, 1984.

Gayle High Pine, "The Non-Progressive Great Spirit," *Akwesasne Notes*, early winter, 1973.

Pat Rodegast and Judith Stanton (compilers), *Emmanuel's Book*, Some Friends of Emmanuel, New York, 1985.

Starhawk, *The Spiral Dance*, Harper and Row, New York, 1979.

Merlin Stone, *Ancient Mirrors of Womanhood,* Beacon Press, Boston, 1984.

Luisah Teish, *Jambalaya: The Natural Woman's Book of Personal Charms and Practical Rituals*, Harper and Row, New York, 1985.

Jane Wagner, *The Search for Signs of Intelligent Life in the Universe*, Harper and Row, New York, 1985.

Barbara Walker, *The Crone Woman of Age*, Wisdom and Power, Harper and Row, San Francisco, 1985.

Barbara Walker, *The Women's Encyclopedia of Myths and Secrets*, Harper and Row, San Francisco, 1983.

Full Circle Workshops offers a series of cassette tapes, including recordings of some of the meditations, exercises and visualizations from *The Inner Dance*.

Inner Dance Tapes

1. Inner Dance Talk
   Earth and Sky Meditation

2. Healing the Inner Child
   Forgiveness Meditation

3. Lovers and Warriors Talk
   Lovers and Warriors Meditation

4. Inner Dance Physical Exercises

Mother Wit Tapes

1. Self Healing
   Inner Self

2. Mother Wit for Children
   Healing Stars
   The Friend Inside

Tapes can be ordered through Full Circle Workshops, Inc. RFD #3, Amherst, MA 01002

About the Authors

Diane Mariechild, M.A., is a mother, psycho-spiritual counselor and a ritual-maker. She is co-founder, with Shuli Goodman, of Full Circle Workshops, Inc. Diane and Shuli travel and teach throughout the United States, Canada and Europe.

Shuli Goodman, M.A., has been trained as a psychotherapist. Her deeper calling is that of a ritualist and singer of sacred songs.

Bonnie Novakov-Lawlor is an acupressurist, a dancer and a teacher of dance and movement awareness in Amherst, Massachusetts. Her background includes the study of Classical South Indian dance as well as psychic studies with graduates of the Berkeley South Psychic Institute.